General Editor
DR ENZO ORLANDI

Text by
MARIO LEPORE

Translator
JULIA SHAW

ISBN: 0-517-163055

Printed in Italy by
Arnoldo Mondadori Editore - Verona

THE LIFE,
TIMES
AND ART OF

REMBRANDT

CRESCENT BOOKS · NEW YORK

Rembrandt's work consists largely of portraits, perhaps because he had an extraordinary gift for portraiture and perhaps because the demands of the society in which he lived coincided exactly with his own particular inclination. Apart from commissioned portraits, there were many friends who willingly posed for him in the sumptuous costumes and strange head-dresses which so appealed to his taste for the exotic. His beloved family, too, was a rich source of inspiration for him. Below left: portrait of his mother in an oriental turban (1631). Below right: probable portrait of his father in an embroidered cloak (also 1631). Bottom: portrait of his sister Lijsbeth.

THE MILLER'S SON FROM LEYDEN

To this day a little street called the Weddesteeg which overlooks the Galgewater, a branch of the Old Rhine, can be seen in Leyden. In 1600 there was a mill facing this little street. Its owner was Harmen Gerritszoon who took his surname, van Rijn, from the name of the river. He and his wife Neeltje Willemsdochter van Zuytbrouck had seven children, five sons and two daughters. When their fifth son was born, on July 15, 1606, his parents gave him the unusual name of Rembrandt although they had chosen popular names of the period for their other children: Gerrit, Adriaen, Willem, Cornelis, Machteld and Lijsbeth. Perhaps this unusual name was a reflection of the miller's hope that, now he had achieved moderate wealth his youngest son would take up a career which would improve the family's social position. In fact while Gerrit became a miller like his father, Adriaen a boot and shoemaker, Willem a baker like his mother's father and Cornelis an artisan, Rembrandt was sent to school and, at fourteen, on May 20, 1620, was entered at the recently-founded but already famous Leyden University. Perhaps his parents hoped he would become a pastor or a lawyer. But the boy showed no inclination to be a scholar. Indeed when, much later in life, Rembrandt went bankrupt the inventory of his possessions showed that he owned a valuable collection of works of art and curiosities purchased with great care and at considerable expense, but very few books. Among these few, however, were copies of the Old and New Testaments. Rembrandt inherited from his mother a love for the Bible and that profound religious sense which permeates his paintings of sacred themes. The sight of his mother reading aloud from the Bible must have made a strong impression upon him, for he portrayed her as the prophetess Anna reading, in a painting now in Vienna. The family atmosphere of affectionate warmth and kindliness which surrounded Rembrandt ensured that, in spite of his imaginative disposition and love for the exotic and luxurious, he remained at heart a simple man who was an affectionate son and brother and later a loving husband and father. His desire to become an artist became apparent very early, and although his father may have had other plans for the boy he gave his approval.

Left: portrait of his mother, sometimes referred to as "Old Woman with a Walking-stick", painted in 1639 (Kunsthistorisches Museum, Vienna.) Below: probable portrait of his brother Adriaen (Louvre). Bottom: probable portrait of his father in an iron necklet, 1629, called "The Aged Warrior" (Hermitage, Leningrad).

Above: "The Surrender of Breda" by Diego Velásquez. The composition and originality of the painting are interesting, as are its realism and beauty. Spinola was a Genoese banker who became a soldier after long sieges on Hertogenbosch, Maastricht and Breda, but he was recalled to Italy and his victories were all to no avail.

Opposite page, top: Philip IV in hunting clothes in a portrait by Velásquez. The responsibility for settling the Dutch problem left to him by his father Philip III, who in 1609 had already drawn up a treaty with the United Provinces approving their final independence, fell to this Spanish King who had a very troubled reign.

Near picture, right: portrait of Frederick Henry of Orange-Nassau. Far right: his brother Maurice, his predecessor as "stadtholder" (ruler; the title formerly meant "viceroy") of Holland and Zeeland, who died suddenly in 1625 while marching against Spinola and his Spanish force, which had attacked the Dutch frontier towns.

THE LONG NETHERLANDS UPRISING

One of the masterpieces of the great Spanish painter Diego Velásquez, "The Surrender of Breda", can be seen in the Prado, Madrid. It depicts Justin of Nassau, leader of the rebellious Dutch, surrendering the keys of the towns he defended to Ambrogio Spinola, commander of the Spanish forces sent to suppress the Netherlands revolt. The painting gives the impression that this was a decisive event. In fact, however, the surrender of Breda was only one of many episodes in the long and sometimes savage revolt of the Netherlands which at that time included most of Belgium and Holland. Charles V gave sovereignty over the Netherlands to his son, Philip II, in 1555. The population was for the most part Catholic but in the Dutch provinces which were nearest to Germany the Calvinist and other Protestant churches found support, particularly from the merchants and financiers who controlled the activity of the great ports, from a large part of the powerful land-owning class and from the working class. The peaceful co-existence of many different religious elements which resulted both from deep-seated mutual tolerance, and from the growing prosperity of the country could have continued if Philip II had not disturbed the delicate balance as much by his odious taxes as by his desire to extend the power of the Inquisition. The Dutch nobility finally rebelled, supported by the Protestant provinces, and the religious struggle increased their desire for independence. The long and bloody struggle which began in 1555 came to an end in 1648 after many successive battles and diplomatic treaties. With the wealth of their merchants, their ship-building skill and their experience in the training of seamen, the Dutch had built up a powerful navy. On October 27, 1639, in the "Battle of the Dunes" in the Straits of Dover Admiral Tromp routed the Spanish Armada. The Spanish were then defeated by the French at Rocroi and in 1643 were forced to yield. They recognized Holland's independence in the Treaty of Westphalia, signed in Munster in January 1648. The so-called "Eighty Years' War" came to an end with the victory of the tenacious Dutch who were led, first by William the Silent, Prince of Orange and Count of Nassau, then, when he was killed, by his son Maurice and finally by Maurice's brother Frederick Henry.

Above: Admiral Harpertszoon Tromp's ship "Amelia" at the Battle of the Dunes which finally secured Holland's independence. The Spaniards were no match for the Dutch navy, who trounced them severely in this battle: Tromp sank or routed 68 of their 76 ships. (Detail from a painting in the Greenwich National Maritime Museum.)

Below: Peter Paul Rubens (1577-1640) painted this portrait of Suzanne Fourment; it is one of the artist's most attractive works (Louvre). Bottom left: detail of the painting "The Sick Girl", by Jan Steen (1626-79) (Rijksmuseum, Amsterdam). Bottom right: detail of the famous painting "Woman Reading", by Jan Vermeer (1637-75)

(Rijksmuseum). Opposite: a portrait by Frans Hals (1581-1666), "The Merry Toper" (Rijksmuseum). The famous artist worked in Haarlem and is considered by many to be the best Dutch portrait painter after Rembrandt. He was the painter of smiles and happiness. His brushwork is modern and vigorous. He died poverty-stricken in a workhouse.

A SOCIETY THIRSTY FOR ART

The long struggle against Spain did not weaken the spirit of the Dutch. On the contrary it encouraged them to unite and make great efforts to increase their trade and maritime power. Three years after Rembrandt's birth a treaty was drawn up which, by recognizing Holland's religious and economic independence, temporarily halted the war, and it did not break out again until 1621. Those peaceful years were notable for the growth of a broadly-based religious freedom, particularly in the provinces, and for the consolidation of wealth. This and the military truce produced a climate in which the arts and culture flourished. The seventeenth century was to be the golden age of painting in the Netherlands. If we begin with Rubens, who was born in 1577, and finish with Jan Vermeer, born in 1632, in a period of 55 years we find in chronological order the following great artists: Frans Hals, Hercules Seghers, Jacob Jordaens, Jan van Goyen, Antoon van Dyck, Salomon van Ruysdael, Aert van der Neer, Adriaen Brouwer, Rembrandt van Rijn, Adriaen van Ostade, David Teniers, Gerard Terboch, Jan Steen, Jacob van Ruysdael, and Pieter de Hooch. This is a magnificent company of great masters supported by a veritable army of lesser artists. Rubens, Hals, van Dyck, Rembrandt and Vermeer stand out above all the rest. But if Dutch society seems, in the words of a contemporary writer, to have been thirsty for pictures, the output, as we would call it today, was so abundant that a very large number of artists, even the most talented, had to work hard to earn a barely sufficient living. The Dutch looked for themselves in art and therefore wanted portraits of themselves, their wives and children, and also scenes representing their own life within the home and outside it. They were realists and the paintings they commissioned from their artists were realistic. At that time the influence of Caravaggio's naturalism was being felt outside Italy and it found widespread favour in the Netherlands. Many Dutch painters studied in Italy and on their return brought back paintings in the new style and a knowledge of its techniques. In their turn, Rubens and van Dyck were themselves the ambassadors of the art of the Netherlands, not only in Italy but in the whole of Europe, where their work was widely acclaimed.

Below: "Tobit and Anna with a Kid", painted by the young Rembrandt (1626). The bright colours do not yet blend in complete harmony of tone. "Portrait of a Young Boy" by Jan Lievens and Rembrandt (detail), and, below right: Johannes Orlers, burgomaster of Leyden, in a portrait by P. Dubordieu. Opposite page, above: self-portrait of Rembrandt aged about thirty, now in the Uffizi, Florence. An early example of his 100 or so self-portraits, it is one of the few paintings by Rembrandt to be found in Italy. Below: H. van der Burgh's "Promotionsumzug", an examination ceremony which was held at Leyden University in the second half of the seventeenth century.

REMBRANDT ABANDONS HIS STUDIES FOR ART

At the time of Rembrandt's birth Leyden was a flourishing town with an important textile industry. It had approximately 80,000 inhabitants. When he died in 1669 its population had increased to about 100,000. In 1575 an Academy or University of lasting fame was founded. In less than five years this university had become so renowned throughout Europe that among its 400 students were many who had come from other countries, for example René Descartes, Théophile de Vian and Guez de Balzac from France. It was a great centre of culture and free-thinking. Rembrandt's introduction to the celebrated academy was not, however, a happy one. The boy learned little and attended his lectures unwillingly, taking every opportunity to draw on spare scraps of paper. Finally he announced that he wanted to be a painter. After much reflection his father consented. If the boy had talent why should he not dedicate himself to art? Hitherto painting had been considered a normal career for a craftsman. It did not have the aura of remoteness and mystery which surrounded it later, and particularly in the romantic nineteenth century, among the middle and lower-middle classes. Rembrandt was therefore taken away from the university and sent as an apprentice to the painter Jacob Isaac van Swanenburch who had lived for a long time in Italy and had returned to Leyden in 1617. Very little is known about Swanenburch and his only remaining paintings show that he was a mediocre artist. But he was probably a good teacher as Rembrandt stayed with him for three years and made rapid and great progress. At the time he was also friendly with a young man a year older than himself. This was Jan Lievens, who had been to Amsterdam to study painting under Pieter Lastman (1583-1633), an artist who enjoyed a deservedly high reputation as we can see from some of his paintings which are in the Rijksmuseum, Amsterdam. Rembrandt and Lievens became friends because of their temperamental similarity and they also worked together. It was certainly Lievens who persuaded Rembrandt to leave Swanenburch and to to Amsterdam to study with Lastman. Harmen van Rijn agreed and his 17-year-old son left for Amsterdam.

THE "ITALIAN" LESSONS GIVEN BY HIS TEACHERS

Rembrandt spent six months in Lastman's Amsterdam studio. Definite proof of this is given by a receipt from Lastman himself, worded as follows: "Received from Harmen, son of Gerrit, of Leyden, the sum of two guilders fifty for having instructed Rembrandt, son of Harmen in the art of painting for half a year". Rembrandt probably also spent a short time in another Amsterdam Studio under Jacob Pijnas. Lastman, like Swanenburch and Pijnas, had lived in Italy and in spite of a preference for the magnificence of classical art inherited from the Carracci, had also studied and absorbed the lesson of Caravaggio's realism and treatment of light. The young Rembrandt hoped to achieve a realism which would be full of human significance as well as being an exact reproduction of an object, and a light which would not merely pierce the darkness and give plastic relief to the composition. In this sense he learned "italianism" from Lastman. The miller's son was sufficiently perceptive to be able to learn the lessons relevant to himself and ignore the inessentials, for he was a painter who preferred to be guided by nature; and prevailing academic fashions meant little to him. In spite of his shortcomings Lastman was able to help Rembrandt just as Swanenburch had helped him from the point of view of technique. Lastman showed him the Italian and the Roman world and the youth could hardly fail to be fascinated by the strange and exotic beauty of its magnificent nobility, its drama and its idealism. Possibly this contact with Lastman would have changed the course of a lesser talent but, as we have indicated, it was useful to Rembrandt in helping to stir his imagination and form his taste. Lastman was not the only influence on Rembrandt. He was also profoundly stirred by his impressions of the great and wealthy city of Amsterdam with her busy port, shops full of wares from all over the world, and men of all nationalities in the streets. Rembrandt's taste for the exotic was undoubtedly stimulated by the sights of Amsterdam. It appears that an outbreak of the plague hastened the young man's return to Leyden early in 1624. He had, however, learned all he could of Italy from his studies with Lastman.

Left: a corner of Amsterdam of Rembrandt's time in a painting by Jan van der Heyden (Mauritshuis, The Hague). Environmental and historical conditions in the Netherlands aided the development of an important school of both great and minor landscape painters who have recorded typical aspects of their country for posterity.

Above: one of the finest self-portraits of the young Rembrandt painted in 1629. Although small, like an earlier but similar self-portrait, it has great expressive power derived from the shadowed eyes and the masterly technique. It is in the Pinakothek, Munich.
Below, far left: "Christ and the Canaanite Woman" by Rembrandt's teacher, Pieter Pieters Lastman. The Italian influence is evident in this work especially in the formality of the composition and the drawing of the figures (Rijksmuseum, Amsterdam). Left: "Tobit's Sons Take Leave of their Father", formerly attributed to Rembrandt, later to his school (Hermitage, Leningrad).

13

REMBRANDT BEGINS BY WORKING WITH LIEVENS

Opposite: Rembrandt's "Balaam's Ass". The painting is remarkable for the brilliance and variety of the colour and for its naturalism. It is now in Paris (Musée Cognac Jay). In his "St. Paul in Prison", below left, the painter abandons variety of colour for a greater unity of style. Below centre: "Self-portrait" by Gerrit Dou, who at fifteen was already a pupil of Rembrandt (Gemäldegalerie, Berlin). Below right: "The Miser", a work of the young Rembrandt in which Caravaggesque echoes still persist in the effects of the candelight. Bottom: "An Old Woman", also known as "Rembrandt's Mother", by Gerrit Dou (Rijksmuseum, Amsterdam).

Rembrandt met Jan Lievens again in Leyden. He was a dyer's son and his background, ideas and view of life and art were similar to those of Rembrandt. The two worked together on several paintings. This is not surprising for at the time artists in Holland and elsewhere often worked together. In the Rijksmuseum there is a head of a youth bearing the signatures of the two artists and it is thought that Rembrandt put the finishing touches to his colleague's painting. Their two signatures also appear on the painting of an old man's head in the Museum at Schwerin. Some of Rembrandt's youthful works have also been attributed to Lievens by certain experts. The two friends worked hard but genius must reveal itself and when, from 1626-27 Rembrandt painted "Balaam's Ass", "St. Paul" and "The Miser", Lievens had already been left behind. In spite of their faults and the obvious Italian influence, traceable to Lastman, these paintings already reveal originality and progress towards a distinctive style, particularly in their treatment of light and shade. In these paintings the strong chiaroscuro is reminiscent of Caravaggio as is the naturalism of characters and attitudes. The colour values, however, with their accent on cool, clear colours, are not Caravaggesque but have a broadly Italian flavour. Above all, in the vigorous composition "Balaam's Ass" we see Rembrandt's imaginative power in depicting Biblical scenes.

REMBRANDT'S FIRST WORKS FIND FAVOUR

Rembrandt's first paintings found favour in Leyden where the connoisseurs already considered him to be a master. Johannes Orlers, former burgomaster of the town, in the second edition of his book *Description of the Town of Leyden* (1641) devotes almost a page to Rembrandt. He was the painter's first biographer and all his other biographers, including the modern ones, have based their work on his comments. After discussing his birth, education and first visit to Amsterdam, Orlers says, "When he had been there (Amsterdam) for about six months he decided to set up his own independent studio and so great was his talent that he became one of the most famous painters of the century. As his work pleased the inhabitants of Amsterdam who commissioned many portraits and other paintings he decided to leave Leyden for Amsterdam. He therefore left this town about 1630 and settled there where he still lives in 1641." (A portrait of Orlers by one of Rembrandt's contemporaries, P. Dubordieu, appears on page 10.) When Orlers wrote these words the artist was little more than thirty, but shortly after his return from Amsterdam his work began to be widely appreciated in Leyden. Probably he established his first studio, with Lievens, in his father's house. But as he became more important he probably had to move from there. We know, in fact, that his reputation grew so swiftly that in 1628 the young Gerrit Dou of Leyden came to him for instruction in painting. Arent Buchel, in a note to a work in Latin, *Res Pictoriae*, written about 1628, says that "the miller's son of Leyden is held in great esteem," and then adds cautiously, "but this is premature." This was quite different from the enthusiastic opinion of Orlers ten years later, but Buchel nevertheless notes that Rembrandt was already very well-known among his fellow citizens. Probably his high reputation was due to the popularity of his religious paintings which were appreciated by everyone in Leyden, a town where there was widespread knowledge of the Bible. His portraits, on the other hand, found an approving audience only among connoisseurs. In fact, although Rembrandt painted many portraits of his acquaintances and self-portraits at this time, as if as exercises, he received relatively few commissions.

Opposite, above: "An Old Man Sleeping". Rembrandt was often drawn to paint old age perhaps because of its distinctive characteristics, perhaps because he was deeply moved by its venerable human qualities. In this painting, which is in the Sabauda Gallery, Turin, there are still slight echoes of Caravaggio, but the subtle and vibrant interplay of light and shade is already typical of Rembrandt. Below: two black-and-white self-portraits of the artist, the first of 1628, the second of 1629, both in the Rijksmuseum, Amsterdam, and showing him in two different moods. Rembrandt's progress from youth to old age is superbly recorded in the self-portraits.

Above: "Portrait of an Artist in his Studio" (Sherman Collection, Zoë Oliver Museum of Fine Arts, Boston). Perhaps his pupil Gerrit Dou posed for this picture. The originality of the composition, in which the light falling from above casts a shadow over the man on the left and achieves a balance by creating a general effect of geometric shapes on the opposite side, is noteworthy. The area of light is extended in the physical and the psychological sense and the greatest quality of the painting is the feeling of space thus obtained. Left: portrait of the artist, bare-headed. This is also an early work.

*Above: "Hermit Reading"; an early
painting by Rembrandt (Louvre).
The theme of tranquil old age recurs
frequently in the artist's work, and
always as evocatively as here. Right:
"The Madonna of the Pilgrims", by
Caravaggio, painted in 1608 for the
Church of Sant'Agostino, Rome.
Lastman, Rembrandt's teacher,
must have influenced this work.
Centrepiece: Rembrandt's "Holy
Family", painted in 1631, now in
the Pinakothek, Munich. The
clear colours used constantly by
Rembrandt for backgrounds enabled
him to achieve subtle degrees of tone
even in shadow. This and later
versions of the same theme are
remarkable for their complete
simplicity and lack of idealization.*

HE RECOGNIZES THE GOOD AND EVIL IN MAN

The great exhibition of Caravaggio's art held in Milan in 1951 revealed the dramatic skill of the Italian master, and his sense of realism which goes far beyond a straightforward representation of natural objects and figures "as they are". Caravaggio, like no other artist before him, used chiaroscuro to give a strong plastic relief to the forms that emerge from shadow into the glare of the intense light to which he exposes them. This new technique found more followers abroad than in Italy, and Rembrandt, in his turn, absorbed its lessons from his teachers who had studied in Italy. But he was a genius with his own individual vision. The difference between Carabaggio and himself grew more marked as Rembrandt's personality matured. We do not know to which of the Protestant churches Rembrandt belonged, but quite obviously he was a man of profound spirituality with a deep sense of religion. He shows an exclusive interest in Man, but he looks at him with a full awareness of his good and evil qualities. He did not merely reproduce the physical appearance of reality. He could see and reveal hidden beauties even in an apparently hideous face, just as he could show the greater virtues underlying an already noble countenance. Those, therefore, who praised the serene modesty and immediacy of Rembrandt's work but give the name realism to what they considered to be his inability to represent beauty, have not understood that he created, not beauty in the classical sense, but an entirely new, innter beauty. His chiaroscuro became his main means of self-expression but the definition between light and darkness is not rigid, as in Caravaggio's work. Rembrandt's shadow is not all-enveloping darkness but has a subtle, hidden life of its own. The transition between darkness and light becomes increasingly imperceptible until it shades into a warm, golden glow, vibrant with colour in which people and objects are revealed. Leaving aside the arguments as to whether Rembrandt's darkness is more significant than his light, whether his figures emerge fully from the shadow or are always on the point of being enveloped by it, it can be said that Rembrandt's "re-invention" of chiaroscuro depends on his inner vision and his spiritual awareness.

In the "Rape of Ganymede" painted in 1636, below, the style is ironic, as if the artist found this pagan legend about a beautiful youth quite unbelievable. An eagle has seized the clothes of a typical Dutch boy and, clasping them in its beak and claws, is carrying him off. The terrified child has a very natural expression of fear and is screaming.

Opposite, above: three portraits which show Rembrandt's unusual psychological insight and his passion for noting details of character. They are "Head of an Old Man with a Gold Cross" and "Lieven Coppenol" (both in the Kassel Museum) and, far right, "Young Man in a Turban" (Royal Collection, Windsor).

THE CLASSICAL WORLD HAS LITTLE INTEREST FOR REMBRANDT

Rembrandt learned from his teachers some of the Caravaggesque precepts and developed, in an original manner, those which were relevant to his own style. He was also fairly well acquainted with the Italian art of his time and of preceding centuries, and with classical antiquity, from the works of other Dutch artists who had stayed in Italy for long or short periods; from his own collection of engravings, many of which reproduced old and new works of art, attractive views etc., and finally from Italian paintings brought back to Holland. However, although he was influenced by Caravaggio, the others interested him only up to a certain point, and often not at all. In some of his paintings there is a vague echo of Titian, Raphael or some other painter but these are fortuitous similarities, not true similarities of style. Rembrandt's expressive power was acquired gradually, largely as a result of his observation of reality. He never had any desire to visit Italy; in fact, his was an anti-classical spirit. Theorists of art such as van Baburen, Crabeth and others were subsequently to condemn him erroneously for this, and the German von Sandrart says in his *Teutsche Academie*, that Rembrandt achieved great artistic beauty despite not having been to Italy, and he criticizes him as an uncultured man with no knowledge of the theories of art. If Caravaggio definitely turned his back on the classical world which Rome offered for his admiration, Rembrandt never wanted to know it. When, by chance, he treated a classical subject he did it in a totally unexpected way; the hallmark of the true genius is his new and subtle interpretations of old themes. His imaginative treatment of some themes was, perhaps involuntarily, a little ironic in its realism, as in the "Rape of Ganymede" (State Museum, Dresden). Or else he allowed himself to be carried away by his fanciful imagination and feeling for the exotic which was stimulated by the cosmopolitanism of the Amsterdam where he lived, and by his daily contact with the inhabitants of the picturesque Jewish quarter of the city, where he lived for a long time. Perhaps the contrast between Rembrandt's fundamental realism and his impulsive imagination could be interpreted precisely as an anti-classical temperament which gave him a preference for the picturesque.

Below: "Rape of Proserpina". This lively composition was probably painted about 1633, a year after "The Anatomy Lesson," as it shows a marked resemblance to other works of Rembrandt's first years in Amsterdam. The Eastern feeling of the chariot, the landscape and the atmosphere have little in common with classical styles.

PROSPERITY IN AMSTERDAM

Rembrandt's father died in 1630 and the artist made his home in Amsterdam the following year. The city, which had been free from Spanish domination since 1578, was largely Protestant but as there was no religious intolerance many people who had elsewhere been persecuted for their various faiths had sought shelter there. About half of Holland's 3,000,000 inhabitants cultivated the land, some of which was gradually being reclaimed from the sea and enclosed by dykes. The other half were town dwellers. In 1630 Amsterdam had 130,000 inhabitants and by the time of Rembrandt's death there were 200,000. Most of the Dutch fleet of 16,000 ships, about a million tons, which included 1,500 ships fitted for herring fishing, were based on the port of Amsterdam,

the most important in Europe and then at the height of its power in every sense. Fishing, mining, metallurgy, textiles, sugar-refining and brewing were the industries which made the hard-working, enterprising Dutch people wealthy. The overseas trading of the Dutch East Indies Company also contributed to their wealth, and the Bank of Amsterdam was considered the most powerful financial institution in Europe. In the first half of the seventeenth century the income of the citizens was the highest, per head, in Europe. Political events did not prevent the growth of economic power which in its turn gave rise to a corresponding enrichment of the general way of life, particularly among the upper classes who if they maintained, as Descartes remarked, the "simplicity of ancient customs" were continually seeking further refinement through culture and art. Rembrandt was widely acclaimed in this city and his work earned him rich rewards. His pupils in Amsterdam each paid him 100 guilders a year. He generally received 500 guilders for a half-length portrait, and up to 1,000 for a Biblical subject. He also earned money from the sale of engravings, and it has been estimated that in the years before his bankruptcy he earned between 10,000 and 12,000 guilders a year. A guilder at the time would have been equivalent to about £4 12s 6d today.

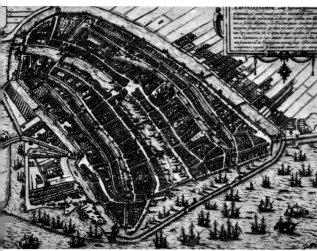

Opposite: The Old Town Hall, Amsterdam, in a painting by Pieter K. Jansz Saenredam. This page, top left: drawing by Rembrandt, of 1652, showing the ruins of the same building after it had been destroyed by fire. This sketch is now in the Rembrandtshuis (Rembrandt's house), today a museum. Centre: plan of Amsterdam of about 1600. Bottom left: the Amsterdam flower market in a painting by Berkheyde. The Dutch were, and still are, passionately fond of flowers, particularly tulips, which were first introduced into Holland, from Turkey by way of Vienna, in 1571. They created new types of the "tulipan" by means of judicious crossing of strains and other means, and the most sought after and rare specimens fetched incredible prices, amounting to thousands of guilders. The aristocracy and middle classes would go to any lengths to obtain them and the great tulipomania of 1634-7 required government intervention. The cultivation of tulips has long since been a source of income and today Holland, the world's largest exporter of tulips, produces some 4,000 million tulip bulbs annually. Even now, although times have changed so greatly, this national flower arouses great enthusiasm. Above: "The Doctor's Visit" by Jan Steen (1626-79). Such 'interiors' were very popular among the home-loving Dutch. Apart from their historical value they often had considerable artistic merit.

REMBRANDT MEETS AND MARRIES SASKIA

It seems that Rembrandt decided to leave Leyden for Amsterdam not only because of the greater prospects offered by the city, but also because he knew that he was shortly to be entrusted with an important commission. The date 1632 which appears on his first masterpiece, "The Anatomy Lesson of Dr. Tulp", supports this theory. Having received his share in the estate of his father, who died on April 27, 1630, Rembrandt, accompanied by his sister Lijsbeth whom he loved dearly, arrived in Amsterdam one year before his "Anatomy Lesson" was completed. Before leaving Leyden he had come to an agreement with an Amsterdam art-dealer, Hendrick van Uylenburch, who knew him and had already bought several of his paintings. Rembrandt apparently went to live in his house. Through his business Uylenburch knew both patrons and artists and Rembrandt made many valuable acquaintances while staying with him. Most important of all, however, he met there the woman he was to marry four years later. This was Saskia van Uylenburch, daughter of Rombert van Uylenburch, burgomaster of Leeuwarden, a small town in Friesland. After her father's death she had come to Amsterdam to live with her uncle. The two young people were drawn to each other first by sympathy, then by love. We know the date of their engagement from a few lines written beneath a sketch of Saskia, (one of the rare examples of Rembrandt's handwriting) which say: "This is a drawing of my future bride when she was twenty-one years old, the third day after our engagement, June 18, 1633." Saskia's marriage to a painter who was also a miller's son, was considered a misalliance by most of her family but Hendrick van Uylenburch supported them and they were married on June 22, 1634. Saskia brought a rich dowry of 42,200 guilders, and, as we can see from the many portraits of her, she was also a beautiful young woman. The newly-married couple stayed with Saskia's uncle until, at the beginning of 1636, they rented a house at No. 20, Nieuwe Doelenstraat. They later lived in another house in Binnen Amstel known as the "Confectioner's Shop" (*die Suycker-backerij*), and in 1639 they finally bought a house in Breestraat for 13,000 guilders. This house is known to this day as the Rembrandtshuis.

Top: silverpoint portrait of Saskia drawn by Rembrandt three days after their engagement (Gemäldegalerie, Berlin). Above: portrait of Titus van Rijn, the only son of Rembrandt and Saskia to survive beyond childhood. He was their fourth and last son and was born in 1641. Rembrandt painted many portraits of him.

Opposite page: "Saskia Wearing a Feathered Hat", one of Rembrandt's most beautiful portraits of his wife. Probably painted in 1634 it belongs to his first Amsterdam period which lasted from 1631-6. It is majestic and elegant, with a slight Rubensesque flavour, very beautiful colour and great delicacy of technique (Kassel Museum).

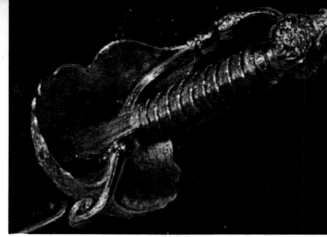

Below left: detail of the head of Saskia van Uylenburch wearing pearl earrings and a little cap upon her burnished brown hair. The harmonization of the dark colours with the warm tones of Saskia's skin and hair is exquisite. Below right: the painter's hand holding a glass of beer, a magnificent pictorial detail.

Right: Detail of Rembrandt's sword hilt, an example of acute observation and technical ability. Opposite page, top: the complete painting. The composition, with the movement of Rembrandt's arm in the foreground and the beer glass acting as a vertical focus between the two heads, is both lively and balanced.

Below: detail of Rembrandt's head. He exudes gaiety and youthful confidence in the potential of life, art and married love. Rarely do we find this mood expressed in such a lively manner in other self-portraits. The plumed hat frames his head elegantly and creates a shadow which gives plastic relief to the illuminated part of the face.

REMBRANDT'S LOVE OF ELEGANCE AND LUXURY

The famous painting in the Dresden Gallery called "Rembrandt and his Wife Saskia", must have been painted at the end of 1634. The feeling of joyousness which animates it shows an aspect of Rembrandt's temperament which he did not generally emphasize. This was his good-natured gaiety, and almost rustic quality, which nevertheless contributed to the love of life and interest in Man on which his realism is based. Later, when dramatic events, such as Saskia's death and his own financial crisis, overwhelmed him we see another Rembrandt, an embittered, distracted man, with whom life has dealt severely; his dark, withdrawn expression suggests that sorrow which gave his later works their gravity and their maturity. But here he is, in the flower of his youth, crowned with success and full of optimism. He is, as we would say, letting himself go, and revelling in his gaiety and his passion for elegance, luxury and sumptuous "disguises". He is allowing the imaginative power which accompanied his sense of realism throughout his life to take control. One could say that he loved reality intensely and idealized it, but not in the classical manner. He looked for qualities that fascinated him in reality which he recreated through this fascination. This double portrait of the painter and his radiant young wife is in essence a portrayal of love, an intimate moment of joy for a newly-married couple. Rembrandt has shown himself as an officer – the influence of the revolt against Spain on a taste for all things military which was prevalent in Holland at the time would repay study – and Saskia is wearing a beautiful dress and many jewels. She is sitting on her husband's knee and he holds her by the waist and turns to face the onlooker while raising a glass of sparkling ale as if in a toast. The dashing yet precise technique of this painting, its colour, harmony and composition are all noteworthy but it is also valuable in giving an idea of the costume and manners of the period. It also gives a possible explanation for the fact that Rembrandt's marriage to a wealthy woman of a higher social position than himself was one of the root causes of his bankruptcy. For although he earned a great deal of money he may have spent it too lavishly in order to live up to his wife's social standing and way of life.

IN SASKIA HE SEES
THE IMAGE OF BEAUTY

We know of seven or eight portraits of Rembrandt's mother, twelve of his sister Lijsbeth, five of his brother Adriaen's wife, but there are many more, painted, sketched and engraved, of Saskia. She was his favourite female model whom he transformed as the subject demanded. This preference for Saskia as a model was not only because he loved her but also because her appearance, her qualities of magnificence and splendour, corresponded to his ideal of feminine beauty. Those critics of the time who, steeped in literature and classical ideals, criticized him for a lack of awareness of beauty were themselves mistaken in not realizing that the concept of beauty is governed by conditions which vary according to period, civilization and country. Rembrandt's taste was, in fact, seventeenth-century Dutch taste. The Flemish artist, Rubens, in spite of his very different education and life, painted women who were basically of the same physical type as those of the Dutch artist. They were handsome, shapely creatures with clear skins and fair or brown hair. In Rembrandt's paintings their fair northern appearance takes on a warmer, more intimate quality. He was able to render this kind of beauty without having to sacrifice any pictorial advantage, rather exploiting his skill with light and colour to enhance it; thus he infused it with a rich vitality and an intense emotional expressiveness, and so was able to describe the simple domestic reality without losing the spiritual one.

Opposite, far left: "Portrait of
Saskia with a Red Flower", (State
Museum, Dresden). This is the last
portrait finished while Saskia was
alive. The artist has captured with
loving perception the uncertain smile
flickering on her lips and the
timidity of her attitude. Opposite,
centre above: full-face portrait of a
pensive Saskia which appears above
a woman's head in profile, in a
drawing of 1637. Centre below:
"Susanna at her Bath", painted
in 1647 (Gemäldegalerie, Berlin).
Above: "Danae" (1636)
(Hermitage, Leningrad),
considered by some to be one of the
most beautiful paintings in existence.
The theme did not inspire Rembrandt
to create a mythological or classical
picture. There is a feeling of surprised
intimacy and warm life in the naked
woman, so reminiscent of Saskia, who
lies, bathed in light, on her soft couch.
The traditional stream of gold,
depicting Zeus, is absent here but the
painting is full of golden tones
reflected in the figures and the
draperies. Left: details of the portrait
"Soldier and his Wife" (Buckingham
Palace) and of "Susanna" (Bonnat
Collection, Paris).

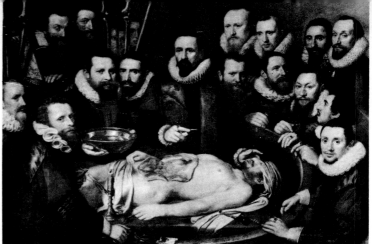

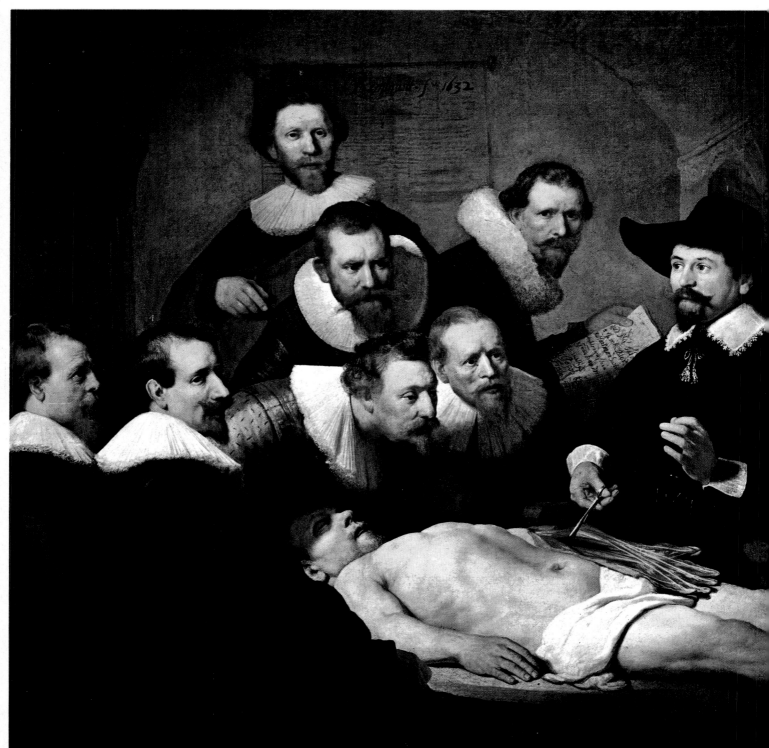

THE IMPORTANCE OF "THE ANATOMY LESSON"

Rembrandt received a warm welcome from the rich bourgeoisie of Amsterdam. He was able to adapt his portrait-painting technique to suit his buyers' somewhat traditional taste. They liked the work of Thomas de Keyser and other similar portrait painters. It was probably because Rembrandt succeeded in pleasing the public that he was given the opportunity to paint an important group portrait "The Anatomy Lesson of Dr. Tulp", which was to be a masterpiece. Rembrandt was probably not surprised to receive this commission for, if the story is true, one of his reasons for moving to Amsterdam was his belief that he was shortly to be entrusted with an important task. Whether or not this is true, he was given this order by the Guild of Surgeons whose principal at the time was Dr. Nicholas Tulp. Although the group portrait was a typically Dutch form of pictorial record, revealing their tradition and their mentality, there are plenty of examples in other countries. These groups, although a fairly recent innovation, had become an established custom by Rembrandt's time. The various city guilds commissioned the best artists to paint them and the theme of the anatomy lesson had already been treated by other artists. Compared with previous efforts by other artists, Rembrandt treated the subject in a novel and very effective way. The light shining on the pale corpse, which lies in the middle of the group, makes it the centre of attention, as indeed it should be, and then leads the eye up to the figure of the doctor. It is only after this that one comes to the rest of the group which, arranged in a classical triangular composition, is of secondary importance to the corpse and to Tulp. The recent cleaning of the picture has revealed a greater sense of spatial unity and also a more lively and finely balanced interplay of colour in the contrast between the yellow-green tones of the corpse and the warm colours of the men's faces, which are linked together by subtleties of tone and chiaroscuro. By focusing light on the corpse, giving it a prominent position and placing it diagonally, Rembrandt was able to place Dr. Tulp and his pupils in a natural position. This enabled him to emphasize effectively the particular atmosphere of the scene and express with force and variety the different emotions of the characters.

Rembrandt painted the group portrait with meticulous truth. The corpse apparently belonged to one Adriaen Adriaensz, a twenty-eight-year-old arrow maker who had been hanged as a criminal on January 31, 1632. The names of five of those present at the lesson are also known. They were sworn members of the Amsterdam Guild of Surgeons. While he depicted the subject with great accuracy Rembrandt was free to position the figures, choose their attitudes and give them individual emphasis by revealing subtle differences of facial expression. The painting is both varied and detailed and the artist has created a taut and intellectual atmosphere.

Above: detail of Dr. Tulp's head. His importance as Principal of the Guild of Surgeons is emphasized by his placing in the group and the light shining on his face and hands.

Below: the penetrating and yet simple portrait of Françoise van Wasserhoven, painted by Rembrandt in 1634 (National Gallery, London). Bottom: "The Four Guardians of the Leper Boy", a good example of the traditional group portrait, painted by Ferdinand Bol (1616-80), who was a pupil of Rembrandt (Rijksmuseum, Amsterdam).

Opposite, top: family group in a typical interior setting painted by Pieter Codde (1599-1678). Painted in 1642, the light in this picture is slightly reminiscent of Rembrandt, but the painting is interesting mainly as an illustration of family life in the Dutch middle class. The period of peace and prosperity caused an abundance of such family portraits.

OPULENCE OF THE DUTCH

For the first half of his life Rembrandt lived in a society which, after bitter strife, had established its own religious, political and economic character and its own traditions. Three years after it began, the revolt of the Netherlands against Spain was interrupted by a lengthy truce which made considerable national development possible. During this peaceful period the wealth of the Dutch increased enormously. Their manners and dress, although still austere for religious reasons, became more magnificent and refined. Expert craftsmen were employed to decorate their homes with sumptuous and elegant materials and furnishings. Without losing their intimate and friendly atmosphere Dutch homes gradually became more comfortable, welcoming and luxurious, and the fashions of the day, as one can see from portraits by Rembrandt, became richer and more elaborate. Prolonged contact with the grandeur of Spain had an obvious effect on the Dutch aristocracy and it also influenced the rich middle class which, while maintaining its decorous attitude, nonetheless became interested in culture and art as indispensable spiritual ornaments for those in a high social position. In the privacy of their beautiful, rich homes the wealthy Dutch led an apparently simple life although they often yielded to the temptation to acquire some beautiful object or enjoy the pleasures of the table. Amsterdam not only presented the picture of energetic business activity which so impressed Descartes in his three years' stay there but it also revealed this more intimate, domestic life. The Dutch "interior" painting, a widely popular genre, shows us typical brick family houses, decorated with coats of arms and friezes, lining the charming old streets and canals of the city. This society, although largely made up of merchants and seafarers nevertheless welcomed artists, scholars, men of letters and printers in such numbers that Amsterdam became known as the Athens of the North. Rembrandt was the greatest portrait painter of this society, and it was natural that he should make some concessions to its taste, but although his paintings are traditional in certain aspects of their composition and treatment, their acute psychological observation makes them unique.

Far left, centre: a fine portrait of a young girl, delicate in tone and lighting, by Johannes Cornelisz Verspronck (1597-1662) now in the Rijksmuseum, Amsterdam.

Below: portrait of the poet Herman Krul, painted by Rembrandt in 1633, noteworthy for its observation of character, its simplicity and restrained elegance (Kassel Museum). Left: portrait of Willem Burchgraeff (1633), a baker and grain merchant from Rotterdam. The light shines full onto the wide lace collar and one side of the man's florid face, casting a deep shadow on the other side. This gives the whole head plastic relief. The eyes, one in shadow, one in light, have a lively expression (State Gallery, Dresden). This was the period in Rembrandt's life when he achieved fame as a portrait painter for his psychological insight and he gained many commissions.

33

EXOTICISM OF THE PORT OF AMSTERDAM

Opposite: "Man in a Gilt Helmet" (Kaiser-Friedrich Museum, Berlin). The warlike motif of the helmet was treated several times by Rembrandt, but in no comparable painting does he achieve such lively effects from the metal. The warm light gives it a golden gleam, and the elegantly worked patterns are rendered in detail.

While studying with Lastman the seventeen-year-old Rembrandt was influenced both by Caravaggio and by the magnificence of Italian Baroque, which was entirely different from Caravaggism and which Lastman had studied in Rome. Amsterdam was at the time a great crossroads of the known world and its trade with far-off countries gave the port an exoticism which also exercised a powerful fascination over Rembrandt. This increasing interest in the splendid and exotic, which contrasts strangely with his profound spirituality, stemmed partly from his delight at the gleam of gold and jewels and the delicate reflection and colour of silks and velvets; from watching the bodies, skin, hair and clothes of the Negroes, Malays, Indians, and Japanese he met in the streets of Amsterdam, and from the strange fruits and products brought back to Holland from overseas by her many thousands of seamen. All these were fortunate visual discoveries but above all they were powerful stimuli to his imagination. The sights of Amsterdam provided an inexhaustible supply of colours and forms to study and use in paintings as a source of novelty and poetry. If we look carefully at his work we see that he chose themes and subjects with which he felt in sympathy. Although he liked to study closely things which attracted him he was able to discriminate. When faced with the picturesque from any source his imagination transformed it, but in a felicitous way. He was attracted by the bizarre but although he was, like others at the time, joined to the Baroque movement, he never treated exoticism as an end in itself. It was merely one element in his imaginative view of the world surrounding him and is thus justified. He later discovered another source of the exotic in the Jewish ghetto. The Jews had come to Holland in great numbers, attracted by the opportunities for trade and the widespread religious tolerance. Rembrandt's contact with the Jewish way of life, which maintained its traditions and secular customs, was the inspiration for much of the oriental flavour which appears in many of his pictures, and particularly in those where he was able to give his imagination free rein. The facility with which he absorbed new people, things and styles from quite alien cultures into his paintings is just one aspect of his extraordinary openness to new and unusual ideas.

Centre, top: a portrait known as "Sobieski", from the strange fur cap. Some think it is a masked self-portrait, others a portrait of a Polish nobleman (Hermitage, Leningrad). Middle: "The Reconciliation of David and Absalom" (Hermitage, Leningrad) and, bottom, "The Rabbi in a Turban" (Chatsworth, Derbyshire); both reveal Rembrandt's love for the exotic East.
Above: the elegant "Portrait of Maria Trip" (Rijksmuseum, Amsterdam).

REMBRANDT'S TRANSFORMATION OF REALITY

The co-existence of a strong sense of reality and a transfiguring imagination is a fundamental characteristic of Rembrandt's art. If we look at the drawings, engravings and paintings we find that he made a careful and minute study of the natural appearance of the perceptible world but constantly treated it in a poetic manner, thus raising it to the level of eternal truth. He looked at reality but recreated it through his own vision, expressing his ideas with a mastery of draughtsmanship and a pictorial skill which he perfected in the privacy of his studio – he had rented a warehouse on the Bloemgracht as a school for his pupils. He evolved his chiaroscuro technique, said to have been inherited from Caravaggio, in an original way which was always appropriate to his own purpose. His progress was gradual. In the first period in Leyden the Italian influence is marked, not only in the emphasis on light, but also the taste for varied compositions and for certain cool, clear colours. In the first Amsterdam period which followed there is a Baroque feeling about his religious compositions, the action is vigorous and there are echoes of Rubens; while in the portraits he began to show a masterly touch which still, however, tended to over-emphasize trivialities. Running from 1636-42, the second Amsterdam period is marked by quieter compositions, the colour is warmer and is beginning to predominate and the brushwork becomes broader and more sweeping. He was perhaps slightly influenced by Raphael and Titian at this time. In the third Amsterdam period which lasted from about 1642-56 and which produced the masterpiece "Christ at Emmaus", his style underwent a profound change in the sense that the emphasis turned to external reality; Baroque vigour disappeared, giving way to meditative, balanced compositions. The religious subjects have great simplicity and yet are full of vitality, while the colour and light grow still warmer and more expressive. Free brushwork was used to define the outline of the pictures. In Rembrandt's work in the years up to his death, known as the fourth Amsterdam period, his vision became more personal; its profound humanity was expressed with a frank and urgent touch. He used very rich, vibrant tones of red, yellow and brown, and with his golden light created a transfiguring and magical atmosphere.

Above: "Hunter with a Bittern" (State Museum, Dresden). The bird is boldly placed in the foreground and its plumage is treated with remarkable delicacy. The hunter looks like Rembrandt himself. Right: Rembrandt's son Titus in a monk's habit (Rijksmuseum). The artist delighted in fantasies such as this; the tone values are very beautiful.

Far left: Saskia as Flora, 1635 (National Gallery, London); Rembrandt often portrayed his wife in magnificent and fantastic costumes. She also appears as the female characters in his religious paintings. Left: "Young Girl with Flowers" also known as "The Jewish Bride" (Hermitage, Leningrad). This is probably Saskia in a different costume. There is little to recall the classical view in this mythological goddess. Saskia as a goddess or a Jewish bride was an excuse for a picture of youth, slightly oriental in tone, which enabled Rembrandt to obtain an unusual richness and variety of colour. Below: detail of the head in the Hermitage painting.

Below: "Simeon in the Temple", 1637 (Mauritshuis, The Hague). The use of chiaroscuro is interesting as is also the subordination of the figures to space and the feeling of solemnity surrounding the great event. Yet the people seem very real, and no doubt many were drawn from the Jewish quarter of Amsterdam. The same subject had already been treated by Rembrandt in 1628-9. Right: "Abraham's Sacrifice" (etching). Opposite, left: the same theme in a painting of 1633; this is rich in dramatic pathos with slight echoes of Rubens. Right: "The Angel leaves Tobias", 1637 (Louvre). The light surrounds the angel like a cloud, leaving the people below in darkness.

GREAT THEMES FROM THE SCRIPTURES

Rembrandt was familiar with the Scriptures from childhood. One can reasonably suppose that readings from the Bible by his mother stimulated his childish imagination, and that the religious element which pervades his sacred paintings had their origins in this seed planted in youth. Certainly he chose to depict the great Biblical themes very early, probably without expecting to reap great rewards from them. Although religious paintings were appreciated in Leyden it was a purely local taste due to the influence of the university and also to the existence, there more than elsewhere, of a deep interest in knowing and discussing the sig-

nificance of the Bible. In any case he knew that the various Protestant churches which predominated in Holland were not permitted to display religious images of any kind. In the Catholic countries many sacred paintings were commissioned but in Holland there were few such opportunities. Paintings of holy subjects were bought for personal edification only and commissions were rare; moreover, collectors were more interested in pagan themes and these were more often requested. Nevertheless, he painted sacred subjects at various times in his life because they fulfilled a certain spiritual need in himself. The great Biblical themes enabled him to use the full force of his imagination, combined with his intense religious and human feeling. Theological controversies were frequent in Holland at the time but he took no part in them. Perhaps, like his mother, he belonged to the Mennonite sect, but basically he defines his own attitude in the reverence, with its uncommon stress on humanity, which permeates his religious paintings. His interpretation of the great Biblical stories achieves a remarkable balance between imagination and expressive style on the one hand, and controlled draughtsmanship on the other.

HIS IMAGINATION IS STIRRED BY STORIES FROM THE BIBLE

Besides the limitations imposed by his own knowledge of the Bible, Rembrandt's choice of subject was often influenced by his desire to treat the less popular Biblical themes, or those previously neglected by other painters. The pictorial possibilities of Biblical stories had been exploited but painters, by tradition, chose to depict a limited selection of the more popular episodes. Rembrandt ignored this tradition. He worked with a very free and imaginative spirit. According to his feeling, the paintings contained an imaginative blending of Baroque, Eastern and Gothic elements, or they might equally recreate a typically Dutch atmosphere. His treatment of the costumes of those portrayed followed the same pattern. He rejected the symbolic and allegorical to remain faithful to the Biblical text, which he interpreted pictorially with all the resources of his imagination and technical skill. His vision is at its highest, most communicative level in the religious paintings and shows itself in his original way of exposing groups of people and single figures to the magical effects of his chiaroscuro. Within a compact composition unusual contrasts are created by unexpected pools of light which disclose infinite depths of space. Precious gems, costly materials, and picturesque clothing and head-dresses also contribute to his harmonious creation of the powerful and dramatic symphonies of form and colour in which he honours the grandeur and eternity of the holy testaments. His new and impassioned expression of an ideal of inner beauty clothed in a shining mantle dominates his vision and makes it unique. He was neither a subtle philosopher nor a man of letters. His religious paintings arose from his reading of and belief in the Old and New Testaments. He was a great artist who, as Muñoz so rightly said, "had his own imaginative and pictorial vision of the world surrounding him, which was based on reality and did not result from some complicated alchemistic process". His profoundly spiritual scenes were a continuous assertion of his faith, confirming the Bible by restating its events in terms of his own experience and imagination. Two centuries later Vincent van Gogh, his tormented compatriot, said, "It is impossible to look at Rembrandt's art and not believe in God".

*Left: "Samson's Wedding Feast",
1638 (State Museum, Dresden).
This lively scene is lighted from left
to right, which underlines the
movement of the whole painting
towards Samson, who sits
expounding a riddle to his guests.
The balance of the painting lies in
the immobile female figure in the
centre.*

*Above: Samson threatening his
father-in-law, 1635. The great
vivacity with which the episode is
depicted arises from the contrasting
expressions on the two faces.
Opposite, below: "Bathsheba",
1654 (Louvre, Paris). The artist
depicts, with simplicity and genius,
the naked body of a beautiful
woman. Perhaps the model was
Hendrickje Stoffels who became his
faithful companion after Saskia's
death. Bathsheba, who appears
thoughtful and resigned to her fate,
holds in her hand her letter for
King David. Left: "Artemis"
(Prado, Madrid). The classical
queen wears a sumptuous costume
and the majesty of her bearing is
accentuated by the small figure on
the left.*

41

"THE NIGHT WATCH"

*Left: "The Night Watch",
1642 (Rijksmuseum, Amsterdam)
painted at the height of Rembrandt's
fame. The critics, particularly
in the late nineteenth century,
have not always been kind to
this picture which is, nonetheless,
a meaningful expression of
Rembrandt's art and of the spirit
of Holland at the time. It is his
greatest and most dramatic
group portrait, employing optical
illusion and using spatial effects
to the full. The painting is also
known as "The Parade of the
Musketeers", and "The Company
of Captain Frans Banning Cocq
and Lieutenant Willem van
Ruytenburch". The militia men
commanded by Cocq, having
taken up their arms, are preparing
to leave the barracks for an
evening parade. This, and the fact
that, before its recent cleaning, the
painting was very dark gave it the
name, "The Night Watch", coined
towards the end of the eighteenth
century, by which it is universally
known. Its present dimensions (12 ft
2 ins × 14 ft 7 ins) are not those
of the original. The painting was cut
down in the eighteenth century when
it was taken from the Guild Hall for
which it had been painted.
Rembrandt was paid only 1,600
guilders for the picture although so
many people appeared in it:
originally there were 31 figures, of
which 16 were portraits. Each of
those portrayed contributed about
90 guilders. This lively and evocative
painting, which contributed in no
small measure to Rembrandt's
already great prestige, now hangs in
the Rijksmuseum.*

"The Night Watch", below, compared with a water colour of 1653 by an unknown artist which was taken from the full-size original. Below these is "The Company of Captain Reynier Reael and Lieutenant Cornelis Michielsz Blaeuw", by Frans Hals and Pieter Codde, 1637 (Rijksmuseum, Amsterdam). Bottom: two other Guild portraits,

the first by Thomas de Keyser representing the Company of Jacob Symonsz de Vries and Lieutenant Dirck de Graeff (1633); the second, by Werner van den Valckert, shows the Company of Albert Coenraetsz Burgh and Lieutenant Evertsz Hulft (1625). Opposite page: details from "The Night Watch".

A SENSE OF MOVEMENT IN "THE NIGHT WATCH"

The military companies for which Dutch citizens volunteered remained active even after the declaration of peace with Spain, and the worthy bourgeois of Holland greatly enjoyed their occasional opportunities for taking up arms. "The Night Watch" was painted in 1642, six years before the peace was concluded, in deference to the tradition that every company should have a group portrait hanging in its own Hall. If we look at a few of these group portraits we can appreciate the new and ingenious technique used by Rembrandt in treating this subject. His figures are not posed, they move in a natural way. As the drum rolls they prepare to fall into line and march. By this realistic treatment the artist was able to create an animated composition on several levels and a great variety of gestures and contrasts of light. As the dimensions of the painting were huge Rembrandt had to adapt and develop his technique. In this painting, with the greatest expressive power at his command, he makes use of heavy and light brushwork as well as a thick impasto applied with a spatula. The various elements merge at certain points giving a sense of life to the picture. With "The Night Watch" Rembrandt broke free from the dangers of immobility, expressing a richness of movement and of nuauce between light and shade which, in some respects, is comparable only with the later works of Titian, Tintoretto and Bassano. Two contrasting colours, yellow and red, form the basis of the painting. The musketeer on the left is in red while the little girl carrying a cock, the heraldic symbol of Captain Cocq, who stands near him, is in yellow. On the right, the lieutenant is in yellow and light blue and behind him stands another musketeer in red. In the centre the figure of Captain Cocq, in black with a red sash, stands out against the colours all around him. The magnificent colour-definition has a throbbing life increased by the feeling of movement which is richly varied in its subtle effects of light and colour on the foreground and background figures. The details on the opposite page show clearly the wealth of different textures in the painting and the striking effects Rembrandt was able to achieve, without at any time slipping into mere virtuosity.

REMBRANDT'S PAINTINGS OF GOSPEL STORIES

Rembrandt, like many other great artists before him, did not write easily. Joachim von Sandrart who published his Teutsche Academie, a book similar to the *Lives* of Vasari, between 1675-79, although praising him, says that he could not read Dutch well. It is interesting to note that Sandart was the only art historian who met Rembrandt. Very few of the painter's private papers are still in existence. There are, however, seven letters to Constantijn Huygens, his friend and admirer from youth who had an important appointment as secretary to the stadtholder Prince Frederick Henry. In the third of these letters Rembrandt alludes to his most important commission for religious paintings: a series of works, representing the Passion, for the Prince. It was the second of his great commissions, the first being "The Anatomy Lesson of Dr. Tulp". "The Night Watch", the "Staalmeesters", and the "Plot of Claudius Civilis" or "Conspiracy of the Batavians" were all given to him later. In his letter to Huygens Rembrandt says that he has completed two of the paintings for the Prince, "The Entombment of Christ", and "The Resurrection", and he asks his friend if they are to be sent to the Prince's home. He also promised his friend a painting, ten feet by eight, as a mark of gratitude for his part in obtaining the commission. The painter carried out this task with great pleasure, perhaps because it was given to him by an important person, and perhaps because the themes were dear to him. In fact the whole series took about fifteen years to complete, and Rembrandt became overwhelmed with work. It is worth remembering that more than two-thirds of his portraits were painted between 1630 and 1640. Yet, even in the midst of this intense creative activity his thoughts often turned to the Old and New Testaments. He knew that the divine and human revelation of their themes, which so inspired his imagination, could be transformed by his own emotional awareness, his sense of movement and light. Guided by an unerring pictorial instinct he created a splendid series of religious works. His first painting inspired by the Scriptures was "Balaam's Ass" of 1626. He confined himself at first to scenes from the Old Testament, and it was not until later in life that he turned to the Gospels for inspiration.

Opposite: "The Raising of Lazarus", c.1630 (Howard Ahmanson Collection, Los Angeles). This was one of the Gospel stories which most attracted Rembrandt. He treated it several times, in oils and in engravings, and always sought a new solution to the problems of composition and light offered by the theme. A Caravaggesque echo lingers in the ray of light which breaks through the darkness, dramatizing the raised hand of Christ, who is in the act of bidding the shrouded figure of Lazarus to rise and walk. He appears to be waking from a deep sleep. A typical detail is the sword hanging on the wall, which provides a subtle point of balance.

*Below: "Christ at Emmaus", by Rembrandt, 1648 (Louvre, Paris). The apostles suddenly recognize the risen Christ in their companion of the road who has accompanied them to the inn. The moment is shown with great simplicity and intensity. The halo which encircles Christ's head is emphasized, not so much by its own light, as by the arching shadows behind Him, while the light shining through the window and falling diagonally across the table-cloth throws into relief the figure of Our Lord, who is blessing the bread.
Bottom: "The Meal at Emmaus", by Caravaggio (National Gallery, London). Despite the great attention to detail, this version has a posed, theatrical feeling.*

If, as has been shown, great biblical scenes stimulated Rembrandt's taste for baroque fantasy and an almost oriental exoticism, his interest in dealing with the New Testament was concentrated largely, and realistically, on man. He made extensive use in his work of the countryside and of elements drawn from contemporary life, without abandoning that note of fantasy that is characteristic of him. Rembrandt never did anything that was not suggested to him by his pictorial sense and for that reason he was aware of the different atmospheres of the Old and New Testaments. While maintaining the necessary correlation between the two his interpretations recognize this difference. Christ, for example, is always portrayed with an air of gentleness and kindness which we never see in the Old Testament figures no matter how much human nobility they reveal. The widely varying events in Christ's life, from His birth to his sacrificial death, take place in an atmosphere quite different from that of the Old Testament stories. Not one of Rembrandt's Gospel paintings (even though he depicts the tragedy of the Passion) presents a scene of such savagery and violence as "The Blinding of Samson", painted in 1636, with all its exceptional qualities of movement and colour. The subjects which inspired him were often traditional ones, but he created a new picture of them. He depicted the great and the more intimate scenes. In the latter the spiritual quality, which permeates his realism more deeply as he grows older and constructs his own personal style, rings out clearly in his pictorial language, his harmonization of design and mellow colour, and in his technique. His originality and mastery are most clearly revealed by a comparison between his work and that of others. In contrast to his Baroque and Mannerist predecessors, who inclined towards dramatic representations of the Gospel stories, those same themes treated by Rembrandt have a curiously peaceful atmosphere. There is a deeply meditative quality about many of his New Testament figures, which sets them apart from his other genre paintings. One should look at his "Christ at Emmaus" in comparison with Caravaggio's, or his "Descent from the Cross" beside a painting of the same subject by the school of Rubens.

Below: a "Descent from the Cross" in the manner of Rubens which differs slightly from the one in Antwerp Cathedral (Koninklijk Museum, Antwerp). Rembrandt's version is seen overleaf. Bottom, from the left: "Christ Carried to the Sepulchre" and "Christ and the Samaritan Woman", two engravings by Rembrandt in which the landscape plays a major part.

Above left: "The Holy Family", 1640 (Louvre, Paris), a theme interpreted by Rembrandt several times. In this small painting the serene and poetic scene has as its background a typical Dutch workman's home. Joseph, his back turned, is working at his bench, with the tools of his trade hanging on the wall. Mary and the Child are lighted by the sun which pours through the window, while St. Elizabeth, who is stooping to look at the child, remains in shadow. The affect is to give a realism and a sense of intimacy to a traditional religious scene. This painting is also known as "The Carpenter's Family".

REALISM IMBUED WITH POETRY

e first two works that Rembrandt painted for
nce Frederick Henry of Orange were "The Eleva-
n of the Cross" and "The Descent from the Cross".
the time he felt the need to express strong emotions
a realistic manner through dramatic chiaroscuro
d intense colour. He probably chose to begin his
ies of paintings with these two subjects because he
d studied the human body while preparing for "The
atomy Lesson of Dr. Tulp", observations which
od him in good stead when he came to depict the
dy of the dead Christ. His realism, although acute,
s given a poetic quality by his own emotions and
ep involvement in the subject. He did not hesitate to
resent himself in a work as a sign of his participa-
n in the drama. In one of the paintings now in the
unich Gallery, he portrayed himself standing at the
t of the crucified Christ, wearing a soldier's cap, his
e tormented and his eyes full of anguish. In "The
scent from the Cross" he appears, on the left of the
ture, as the blue-clad figure with his feet on the
lder, who is helping to take down the lifeless body
the Lord. His expression of bitter grief is partially
lden by shadow in the painting but can clearly be
n in an etching of the work. Rembrandt continu-
y analyses himself in his many self-portraits which
ow many nuances of his character. He also ques-
ns his own reaction to great religious events. It
uld have seemed natural if this had happened in the
ars when the events of his own life gave him cause
sorrowful reflection. However, such were the
pth and quality of his feelings, he tried constantly to
d an answer to the question "Who am I?" which he
ver ceased to put to himself even in times of success
d joy in love. In "The Descent from the Cross", a
bject treated by him on other occasions, a ray of
oonlight falling from the night sky onto the Cross
d focussing attention on the blood-stained wood,
d the livid colour of the corpse against the white
roud, create an extraordinary effect which is em-
asized by the shadowy figures on each side. Mary
ls fainting in the darkness. The grave, solitary
ure on the right, wearing a characteristic turban is
rhaps that of Nicodemus.

Opposite: "The Descent from the Cross", 1633 (Pinakothek, Munich). The Cross, in the form of a "T", placed diagonally in the centre of the picture, is the pivot of the triangular composition. The light and movements are effectively concentrated in the upper part nearest the top angle of the triangle.

Above: "The Ascension of Christ", 1636. Christ rises towards the heavens which open to receive Him in glory. The dynamism of the painting lies in the rhythmic movements which develop diagonally upwards and from right to left. The figure of Christ, with raised, outstretched arms bears a slight resemblance to the Mary in Titian's "Ascension" in the Church of the Frari, Venice.

A DRAMATIC TURNING POINT IN REMBRANDT'S LIFE

Opposite: portrait of Saskia painted in 1643, the year after her death (Gemäldegalerie, Berlin). The death of his beloved wife had a profound psychological effect on Rembrandt who felt a desperate loneliness. This somewhat idealized portrait of Saskia is an embodiment of happy memories rather than a realistic picture of her.

Below: notice of the auction of Rembrandt's etchings. Bottom left: detail of his portrait of Jan Six, a friend of the painter and burgomaster of Amsterdam, 1654. This is one of Rembrandt's most attractive portraits. Bottom right: Titus at fifteen, a tender portrayal of adolescence. (Wallace Collection, London).

The year of "The Night Watch", 1642, was also the year of Saskia's death. She died on June 14. On September 22, 1641, their son Titus had been baptized, but Saskia was ill even before the baby's birth. In spite of her husband's loving care her condition grew worse. On June 3 she made her will leaving the sum total of her property to her son. Her husband was to have the interest for life if he did not remarry. No inventory of possessions was presented. (The clause in the will relating to a second marriage was widely used at the time.) Geertige Direx, the widow of a trumpeter, had joined the household as a wet-nurse for Titus during Saskia's last illness. She became fond of the boy and made a will leaving everything to him. When the woman left his service Rembrandt gave her 150 guilders and an annuity of 60, which he later increased to 160. But the widow did not want to leave the house and accused Rembrandt, in the matrimonial courts, of having had improper relations with her; she claimed he should either support or marry her as, so she said, he had promised. Rembrandt denied everything before the court which nonetheless ruled that he should pay the widow a pension of 200 guilders a year. The scandal cost Rembrandt much goodwill. Probably Geertige Direx was moved by the jealousy she felt when, in 1645, a charming young 23-year-old girl, Hendrickje Stoffels joined the household and Rembrandt fell in love with her. They had a son who died on August 15, 1652. There was a great deal of gossip and many of Rembrandt's friends began to avoid him. Hendrickje was reprimanded by the ecclesiastical court for her illicit relationship with Rembrandt and on June 23, 1654, she was barred from taking Holy Communion. This did not, however, discourage either her or Rembrandt. On October 30 of the same year they had a daughter whom Rembrandt called Cornelia after his mother. Perhaps Rembrandt would have married his mistress, but his financial collapse made this impossible. The Breestraat house, bought in 1639, had been partly paid for but the outstanding debt was 8,470 guilders and there were other debts of more than 9,000 guilders. There was no way of paying them. The artist was officially declared bankrupt and his possessions were sold by auction for a fraction of their value.

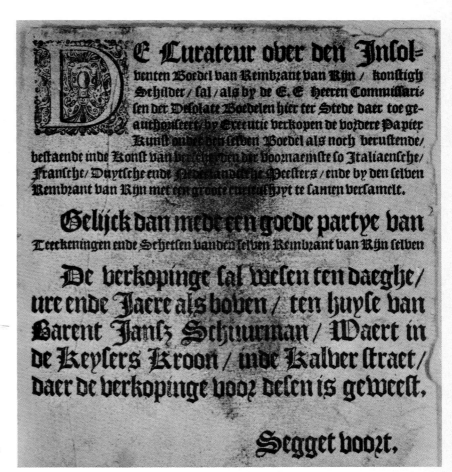

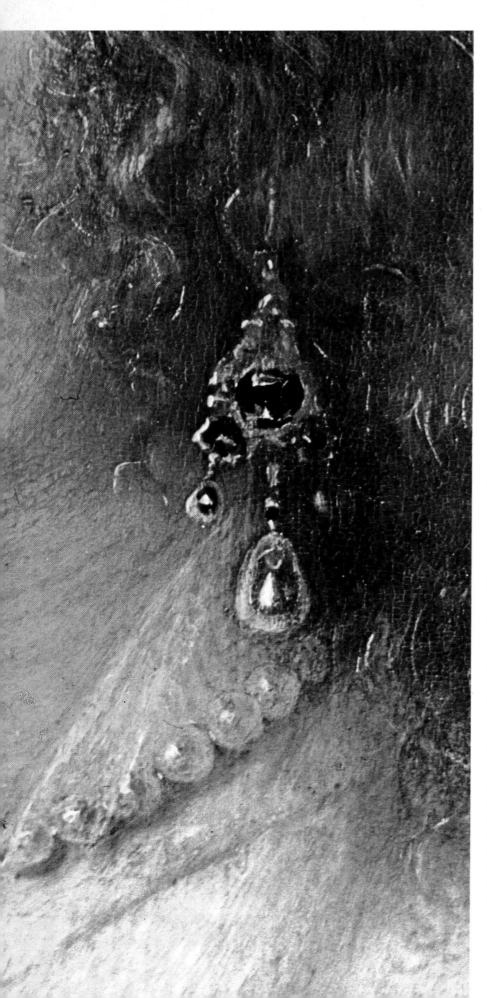

THE SIGNIFICANCE OF THE INVENTORY

Following his bankruptcy an inventory of Rembrandt's possessions was drawn up on July 25-26, 1656. The 20 pages of this inventory show two things. Firstly, that he was an enthusiastic collector, and secondly that most of the money he had spent so freely, until, despite his great earnings, he became bankrupt, had been used to acquire the exotic and precious objects which appealed to his collector's instinct, and that delight in being surrounded by the costly and the unusual which his paintings exhibit. Rembrandt's house contained many treasures, amassed over the years with discrimination by the artist, who frequently visited the Amsterdam auction sales. Unfortunately, Rembrandt's personal financial crisis coincided with national economic difficulties. A few years after their victory over Spain the Dutch found themselves confronting the English, who had become a great maritime power and were challenging the Dutch for domination of the sea. After 1650 the extraordinary prosperity of Holland began to decline, and the people were drawing in their purse strings. Rembrandt's treasures were less attractive to collectors than they might previously have been. He had paintings by Adriaen Brouwer, Lievens, Lastman, Pijnas, Seghers, an important Rubens "Hero and Leander", now in Dresden, paintings by Palma the elder, Moretto, Bassano, and possibly a Raphael Madonna. There were carefully chosen etchings of various types by Lucas van Leyden, Cranach, Raphael, Mantegna, Dürer, Titian, the three Carracci, Reni, Ribera and Tempesta. There were volumes of drawings by Rubens, Jordaens, Mierevelt, Titian, Lastman and Bol; other volumes contained engravings of Turkey, Rome and ancient monuments. There were also about 30 volumes of sketches by Rembrandt himself, and many of his paintings and studies, finished and unfinished. There were also Roman medals, helmets, cuirasses, musical instruments, materials, furs, porcelain from the East Indies, original sculptures and casts, Japanese helmets and many other treasures. There were few books, but among them was a Bible. Also there was furniture, linen and household articles, in all 363 items. It is an inventory which throws light both on Rembrandt's art and the formation of his taste.

Opposite: detail showing a pendant ear-ring from Rembrandt's portrait of Maria Trip. This page, from the left: "The Flautist", by Brouwer (Royal Museum, Brussels) once owned by Rembrandt. Centre: Rembrandt's house, the cause of his ruin, on Breestraat. "Negro with a Bow and Arrows" by Rembrandt (Wallace Collection, London).

Above: a landscape by H. Seghers (Uffizi, Florence). Several works by this painter were in Rembrandt's collection. He was present at an Amsterdam auction sale when the portrait of Baldassarre Castiglione by Raphael, centre left, was sold; he made a sketch of it, far left. The headdress, a feature of the portrait, appealed to him so much that it reappears in more decorative form in an etching, near left, and also in other works.

HENDRICKJE, HIS FAITHFUL COMPANION, STAYS BY HIS SIDE

Above: "Hendrickje Stoffels" (Gemäldegalerie, Berlin). Rembrandt, who was in love with her, painted her repeatedly. She was his model for Bathsheba and Asenet, Potiphar's wife. Here she is in a natural pose, full of life but with a slight air of melancholy. Opposite, in black and white, "Flora", c. 1655 (Metropolitan Museum, New York). As previously with Saskia, Rembrandt used Hendrickje as a model for this latest painting on a previously treated theme. The simplicity of this later, more rustic "Flora" is striking. The harmonization of the colours, the natural pose and the noble grace of the figure, seen in profile, are most attractive.

Rembrandt's house was not formerly divided as it is today. There was a hall leading to a side room, beyond which was another room leading into a back room. An antechamber gave access to a small study containing curios. Then there was a small studio, a large studio, a store for painting materials, a small writing room, a tiny kitchen and an access corridor. Everything was removed from the house, even the half-finished works. No-one came to Rembrandt's aid. He was even abandoned by Six who had admired him sufficiently to commission him to paint a portrait of his mother, a Biblical painting and, later, his own portrait, which is a masterpiece. Rembrandt had also engraved a portrait of Six reading near a window, a landscape showing his country home, and an etching called "Six's Bridge". At that time they were close friends, but Six wrote off the thousand guilders owed to him by Rembrandt and abandoned him. The house was sold for 6,713 guilders. In two auction sales, one in September, 1657, the other in December, 1658, Rembrandt's possessions were sold and realised only 4,964 guilders. From December 4, 1657, the painter had to stay at the Keyserskroon Inn, but he did not finally leave the house until about 1660. Hendrickje Stoffels was the only person to remain by his side. This ordinary, but courageous and sensible woman faced their changed circumstances resolutely. In the new house to which Rembrandt, she, Titus and the baby Cornelia moved in the Rozengracht opposite the Nieuwe Doolhof (now No. 184) she ran the house, was an affectionate mother to both children, a model for Rembrandt and even acted as a picture dealer on his behalf. In fact in December, 1660, she and Titus formed a company to sell Rembrandt's paintings and etchings. In the deeds the artist appears as the manager receiving board and lodging and everything necessary for his life and art in lieu of salary. It appears from the document that Titus paid in an advance of 9,500 guilders and Hendrickje 800. The purpose was to prevent Rembrandt from being further harassed by his creditors who, despite having sold all his possessions, had not yet been repaid in full. On October 27, 1662, Rembrandt was even forced to sell the family tomb; of all his possessions of substantial value it would have been the last to go.

Far left: Geertige Direx, from behind, with the child Titus: a rapid sketch by Rembrandt. Left: The artist in an objective self-portrait which shows his skill as a draughtsman who is capable of grasping a subject and in a few effective and telling lines expressing it truthfully and with understanding.

Top: "Moses Shatters the Tables of the Law" (Gemäldegalerie, Berlin). Left: "Titus Reading", c.1657 (Kunsthistorisches Museum, Vienna). This is one of the most beautiful of the 18 portraits of his son. The concentrated pose of the young man and the subdued colours emphasized by the warm light show the painter's affection.

From top: "Dr. Faustus",
an engraving made between
1652 and 1653; a "Crucifixion"
of 1635, full of movement and
feeling, typical of Rembrandt's
work of the period;
"Rembrandt's Mother in a
Black Veil", 1631. The
subtle interplay of light
and shade is noteworthy.

A GREAT DRAUGHTSMAN AND A BRILLIANT ENGRAVER

Etching is a cutting technique. A layer of wax is spread on a copper plate and the artist draws his design on the wax with a pointed object which penetrates through to the copper. He then pours acid over the plate which eats into the metal and marks it with the lines he has drawn. The wax is removed from the plate, which is stained with ink before being cleaned. The ink penetrates the marks scored on the plate by the acid and the design can now be printed on paper when the plate is subjected to pressure in a hand-press. The operation can be repeated several times producing many copies. Rembrandt used the etching technique and also the method of direct engraving on the plate with a sharp point (dry point). He preferred the latter method in his mature years because he was able to use strong lines, although he used the first method for a long time, being able to draw on the soft wax as if it were paper. For him, etching opened a way to achieve effects he could not otherwise have captured. Rembrandt was a draughtsman of genius and a brilliant etcher, perhaps the greatest of all. The etchings established his reputation as a great religious artist and, so to speak, launched him as a portrayer of Biblical and Gospel stories. His etchings realized very high prices, for example his "Jesus Healing the Sick" which was also known as "The Hundred-Guilder Print" because of the sum paid for it. Although the art of etching already existed before Rembrandt, and particularly in Italy, he established it as an art form in its own right. Indeed his post-1640 works set a pattern for the medium until the time of Goya. In the period up to 1650 he created his most famous etchings; before 1640 they had mostly been reproductions of his own paintings, but after that year they were often original works with a genuine force of poetic and pictorial expression resulting from the black and white treatment and the interplay of light and shade. By using various techniques, for instance etching and dry point together, he attained near-perfection. Such widely differing works as "The Three Crosses", and "Dr. Faustus" are intensely evocative. Rembrandt's last etching was a portrait of the botanist Van Linden (1665).

Left: portrait of Ephraim Bonus, a a Jewish doctor; the date and signature on this etching "Rembrandt f. 1647" are barely legible. Bonus was a friend of the artist. His grave and penetrating expression, austere clothing and his pose, with one hand on the newel, give a feeling of great dignity to the portrait which is entirely appropriate to the sitter's profession. Above: the higest-paid of all

Rembrandt's etchings, "Jesus Healing the Sick" also called the "Hundred-Guilder Print", because an impression of this etching is reported to have been sold for such a sum during Rembrandt's lifetime. The models for the sick could have been found in the Jewish quarter of Amsterdam, which was inhabited not only by the Jews in their curious traditional clothing but also by the poor.

Rembrandt was drawn to these unfortunate victims of fate as much by his interest in the picturesque as by his deep sense of humanity. This full and animated composition has a more or less diagonal movement which divides the area of darkness from the light where the figure of Christ stands out in relief against the dark background, dominating the people clustered round Him.

A LANDSCAPE PAINTER WHO NEVER TRAVELLED

On June 9, 1652, the old Town Hall of Amsterdam was destroyed by fire. Rembrandt came from the distant Jewish quarter where he lived, sat down and sketched the scene before his eyes. Whenever anything struck his fancy, wherether it was a ragged beggar in the street, an animal, a rabbi, Saskia asleep on her bed, Hendrickje at work or Titus playing, he did the same. An artist's sketches reveal much about him when they are used, as Rembrandt used his, as an outlet for his feelings. His landscapes, 14 in all, which are an important aspect of his total work, were mostly executed in the ten years between 1638-48. They were probably based on his sketches and his talent for embroidering reality played a complementary part. But what of travel, the true basis for landscape painting? Rembrandt journeyed the 20 miles between Leyden and Amsterdam, but that is all. Probably, however, those 20 miles of rather flat countryside provided him with enough impressions of rock, trees, bridges, streams and houses to last him a lifetime; the only other sources he used were his impressions of Amsterdam itself, and of the landscapes of other artists which came to his notice. His was a sedentary life. He had to work hard to complete his commissions and otherwise travelled only in his imagination. In the inventory of his possessions, as we have seen, there were volumes of engravings of Rome, Turkey and of classical monuments, which he must have leafed through and contemplated at length, absorbing their atmosphere. In this way he created, from a basis of physical reality, an imaginative, yet credible reality of his own. It was a poetic expression in which man, if he appears, is of secondary importance and, like a tree or an isolated cottage, forms part of the natural landscape. His scenes, in the form of etchings and paintings, began to appear during the 1640s. But, although the landscape was very popular in Holland at the time, Rembrandt specialized in it during one short period only, when he created a number of superb works which vividly present his view of the nature he longed for so passionately.

Opposite, above: the famous etching "The Three Trees", 1643, a hymn to nature in black and white. The trees tower over the men working in the fields and the animals grazing peacefully; on the right a farm-wagon passes over the top of a sunlit hill. Few other artists had Rembrandt's sense of space or could express it with such simplicity. Below: "River Valley with Ruin", 1643-8. In this rather romantic open landscape the ruins provide an unusual echo of the classical world. Perhaps the idea was suggested to him by his reading of the books about Rome which were included in the inventory of his possessions.

Above: "Landscape with Obelisk" (Isabella Stewart Gardner Museum, Boston). Leonardo da Vinci was the first to paint imaginary landscapes. Rembrandt owned some eight paintings and several etched copperplates by H. Seghers, the Dutch artist and fellow citizen who continued the tradition. Here Rembrandt creates a feeling of depth and drama in which the ancient tree, in the foreground, and the storm clouds play their part. The hub of the picture is the tall obelisk which rises from the plain in an oasis of tranquillity. Left: a sketch of a tree-stump, drawn with rapid, strong ink strokes.

61

Below: "Homer", 1663 (Mauritshuis, The Hague). Bottom left: "Ecce Homo", 1663 (National Gallery, London). Christ before Pilate was a theme also treated by Rembrandt in an etching. As always he shunned traditional treatments. Bottom right: "Homer Dictating to a Scribe" (watercolour sketch).

Opposite: "Aristotle Contemplating a Bust of Homer", 1653 (Metropolitan Museum, New York). Don Antonio Ruffo, a rich art-collector, paid 500 guilders for the painting in 1654. He later commissioned companion pieces, a "Homer" and an "Alexander". The painting was sold in America in 1961 for $2,300,000.

Rembrandt looked at the ancient world in the same way as he looked at the Bible. He saw it imaginatively and with his habitual taste for the picturesque, a taste increased by his contact with daily life in the Jewish quarter. He was far removed from Graeco-Roman classicism, both by his slight knowledge of it and by his own temperament, and so it was natural that he should choose to interpret classical themes in a highly personal way. The subjects of pagan antiquity provided him with an opportunity to express his views of contemporary feminine beauty and the venerability of old age, which aroused a deep emotional response in him. His ancient poets and philosophers resemble his prophets and wise men, patriarchs and Biblical kings. In his magnificent water colour of the blind Homer dictating to a scribe there is a strong resemblance to his Abraham in the etching, "Abraham Receiving the Angels". His Pontius Pilate is more like an imaginary Eastern potentate than a Roman consul. Rembrandt was not bound by any conventional plan, but, relying upon his own imagination and pictorial sense, he succeeded intuitively in painting subtle and moving works. The watercolour of Homer, below, shows that only a part of the original painting completed in 1663 remains. Nevertheless its colour, chiaroscuro and acute psychological observation make it seem complete in itself. Although inspired by the famous classical bust of Homer, of which he owned a copy, Rembrandt shows us a living man, who suffers and who is, at the same time, absorbed in his great poetic vision. The same bust of Homer appears in the thought-provoking symbolic painting of "Aristotle Contemplating a Bust of Homer". It was commissioned by an Italian collector, Don Antonio Ruffo of Messina, and, contrary to the view often expressed, proves that Rembrandt's art was appreciated outside Holland. In this painting he probably wished to show that poetry and wisdom, as represented by Homer and Aristotle, together ennoble mankind. A second commission from Don Ruffo, "Alexander", was probably destroyed by a fire in the Messina Gallery; and also a third, of "Homer Dictating to a Scribe", which is shown in this page.

Above: "The Plot of Claudius Civilis" also known as "The Conspiracy of the Batavians" (National Museum, Stockholm). The enormous canvas, about eighteen feet square, in which magnificent lighting effects throw into relief the faces and weapons of the conspirators, was completed and delivered in August 1662. Rembrandt had accurately studied its future position and his technique,

although as vigorous as in "The Night Watch", had been adapted to suit the exceptional size of the painting. This work had been commissioned for the new Amsterdam Town Hall but it did not meet with approval. A more conventional historical painting was required. Rembrandt made several alterations but, a year later, a painting on the same subject by Ovens, a former pupil of

Rembrandt, was hung in its place. It appears that Rembrandt himself cut the canvas down in size. Right: two sketches for "The Plot of Claudius Civilis" which show that the existing fragment was the centre portion of the foreground in the original painting. The background, with its wide arches, was sacrificed. Above right: "The Anatomy Lesson of Dr. Deyman", now in the Rijksmuseum, Amsterdam.

TWO MAGNIFICENT FRAGMENTS

Besides the "Homer" in The Hague there are in existence other fragments of paintings by Rembrandt. These are the "magnificent fragments" of two works, painted in the artist's last period, "The Anatomy Lesson of Dr. Deyman" of 1656, and "The Plot of Claudius Civilis" or "The Conspiracy of the Batavians" of 1662. A knowledge of the preliminary sketches has enabled us to reconstruct the originals. They were important commissions, the second being destined for the Great Hall of the new Amsterdam Town Hall. Despite everything, Rembrandt still enjoyed a high reputation, and once again he had a good deal of work to do. In the "Lesson of Dr. Deyman" the foreshortened body at the centre of the composition is reminiscent of "The Descent from the Cross" of Borgianni, of the school of Caravaggio, or of an earlier work, "The Dead Christ" by Mantegna. The fragment still in existence shows a severity and harshness unusual in Rembrandt's work of the period. The characterization in the painting suggests that he had taken great care to paint exact portraits. In his "Claudius Civilis" the theme of the Batavians' uprising against the Romans was obviously suggested by the recent Dutch revolt against Spain. The conspirators are shown seated round a table by candlelight, swearing loyalty to their leader, whose head-dress and yellow clothing, seen against the dark background, make him the dominant figure and a focus of movement in the composition.

65

DUTCH CIVIC SPIRIT IN REMBRANDT'S LAST MASTERPIECE

In the last years of his life Rembrandt received further important commissions. In 1661 Don Antonio Ruffo of Sicily commissioned an "Alexander the Great" and the following year a "Homer" (possibly the Stockholm painting). In 1669 he also purchased a complete series of Rembrandt's etchings. The artist's last masterpiece was begun in 1662, the year when his "Plot of Claudius Civilis" received an unenthusiastic reception. The members of the Clothmakers' Guild commissioned a group portrait for their Guild Hall. This painting was also known as the "Staalmeesters" and with "The Jewish Bride", painted some years later, surely demonstrates Rembrandt's sublime pictorial genius. In "The Night Watch" Rembrandt broke away from the stereotyped and rigid group portrait, as seen by his predecessors, and created a very expressive painting with a strong military and picturesque flavour, which clearly expressed Dutch enthusiasm in the fight for independence, then the burning issue of the day. In the "Staalmeesters", as Muñoz rightly says, he shows the other face of Holland as revealed in the thoughtful, reflective and peace-loving citizen. Here the five members and their servant seem to be listening to an invisible speaker in front of them. It is a simple, posed scene, but at the same time it is full of life. It has total unity yet each figure can be viewed as an individual. The colour scale, with the warm, red note introduced by the tablecloth, and the golden light which gently brightens the atmosphere and falls upon the grave, benevolent men in black, contributes greatly to the sense of unity of the whole, and to the pictorial life of the painting. One's eye is drawn, by the complex structure and rhythmic movement, towards the central figure of the President, whose position is further emphasized by the stooping figure on the left and the servant in the background on the right. Rembrandt's technical skill is outstanding. So free and vigorous is the style that the painting seems almost to have been created *d'un seul coup*. We see here a splendid example of Rembrandt's ability to observe and analyse reality, of his technical skill and above all, of a creative genius such as has rarely been seen.

Opposite, left: "The Burgomasters of Amsterdam Awaiting the Arrival of Maria de' Medici", by Thomas de Keyser (Mauritshuis, The Hague). Top left: "The Masters of the Guild of St. Luke at Haarlem" (Rijksmuseum, Amsterdam). A comparison between the "Staalmeesters" and these groups reveals Rembrandt's genius.

Above: An infra-red photograph of the third figure from the left, the head of the president, in the "Staalmeesters". Infra-red photographs of this painting and "The Night Watch" disclose the work involved in achieving an apparent fluency of style. The seemingly fortuitous naturalness resulting from the harmonization of the various individual movements in the group was finally achieved only after much revision. Rembrandt experimented on the canvas itself and did not hesitate to paint out one picture and superimpose another. Some of the effects he makes with his material are in fact due to this. The layers beneath the visible surface cannot be seen, and yet they alter the texture and consistency of the paint. Rembrandt often repainted a picture or large parts of it so that the new layer of superimposed colour gave it a richer, more vibrant effect. Many notable art critics have shared the view that this group portrait marked the final development of Dutch national art, and it has been the subject of exhaustive studies.

67

Below: "Old Man with a Red Cap", probably painted about 1655, now in Berlin. The colour is vibrant and the treatment expresses the picturesque qualities of the subject boldly and freely. Bottom: school of Rembrandt, detail from "Portrait of a Man in Armour". Right: "The Slaughterhouse", 1655 (Louvre, Paris).

HIS STUDIO BECOMES A STRONGHOLD AGAINST ADVERSITY

Opposite, far right: "Woman Bathing", 1654 (National Gallery, London). The small painting resembles "Bathsheba". The model was Hendrickje who is here cautiously entering the water, with her chemise raised to keep it dry. The painting gives a charming and intimate picture of a woman who is unaware of being watched.

Misfortunes never weakened Rembrandt's spirit. On the contrary, when his financial crisis was imminent he tended to avoid company and bury himself even more deeply in his work. According to his biographer Houbraken who, although not always reliable, was in this case probably correct, he was a man who contented himself with little, naturally quiet and home-loving despite his well known taste for the exotic, exemplified both in his paintings and his collection of precious objects. His increasing financial problems disturbed him in that he was afraid that all his treasured possessions would be forcibly removed, as in fact happened, and because he saw his loved ones in a precarious position. But he had no fears for himself. This explains why, during the stormy period when his creditors were pressing for payment and his friends were avoiding him, he shut himself up in his studio, as if it were a stronghold able to withstand any adversity, and there, developing and broadening his artistic vision in both form and colour, painted such magnificent pictures as "Bathsheba", which was inspired by his constant and devoted young companion Hendrickje. Heedless of the opinions of buyers, despite his financial position, Rembrandt concentrated on experiments which seemed necessary to him. There is, for example, a group of pictures on which the paint is so thick that, according to Houbraken, a painting placed on the floor could be lifted by the projecting impasto on the nose, modelled so thickly that it might have been a bas-relief. His desire to experiment led him in about 1655 to paint a slaughtered ox, a work which subsequently aroused great interest among the moderns. Any other Dutch painter would probably have treated a similar subject in the form of a still life or "vanitas" as they called it. For Rembrandt this was simply a pretext to paint a monumental form, observed with a powerful and uncompromising realism and transfigured by means of colour and chiaroscuro. Perhaps this most unusual subject may be used to illustrate how he understood the problems of colour and form of every subject in a way that was entirely detached from its literary content, and that his own language had an exclusively pictorial foundation.

HIS PUPILS BECAME OUTSTANDING PAINTERS

The artist Jurriaen Ovens, whose painting took the place of "The Plot of Claudius Civilis", had been a pupil of Rembrandt 20 years earlier. Several former pupils were entrusted with commissions for the new Town Hall in Amsterdam. Even before Rembrandt was asked to do a painting, Flinck, another of his pupils, had done some work for the newly completed building. Rembrandt had about 40 pupils. His first was Gerrit Dou who, at the age of 15, went to Leyden to learn from a master who was perhaps only five years older than himself. Rembrandt taught some of his pupils everything, perfected the technique of others, while a few pupils came to him for one or two lessons only. Of the 40 young men those who afterwards achieved fame besides Dou, Ovens and Flinck, were Jacob Adriaensz Backer (1608-51), Ferdinand Bol (1616-80), Gerbrand van den Eeckhout (1621-74), Carel Fabritius (1622-54), Samuel Van Hoogstraten (1627-78), Barend Fabritius (1624-73), Nicolaes Maes (1634-93), and Aert de Gelder (1645-1727). Most of these, although naturally influenced by their master, developed their own individual styles which eventually differed more and more from Rembrandt's as his own paintings conformed less and less to the taste of the period. Nevertheless something of his influence was passed on by his pupils: Lievens, hardly a pupil, but a friend of his youth who shared his ideas and tastes, and Dou, Bol, Carel Fabritius and Maes, who influenced the work of other artists such as Frans van Mieris, Gabriel Metsu, Jan Vermeer and Pieter de Hooch, and through them perhaps all of Dutch painting. We know nothing of Rembrandt's teaching methods at the lessons he gave in the warehouse on the Bloemgracht, where he taught many pupils in his most successful period. It is interesting, however, to note that even when he was old and lonely several young artists came to him for instruction. Aert de Gelder, born in 1645, was one of these. Probably few of his pupils saw Rembrandt at work because it is well known that he liked to be alone while painting. Dou, however, must have been present while he was working in Leyden if, as is thought, he acted as model for "The Artist in his Studio", which is now in Boston.

INSPIRATION THROUGH PERSONAL GRIEF

The year 1662, when Rembrant painted "The Members of the Clothmakers' Guild", was the year of Hendrickje Stoffels' death; in 1642, the year Saskia died, he painted "The Night Watch". It could be said that these masterpieces were achieved at the cost of great grief. Hendrickje, a homely, gentle and courageous woman who had instinctively understood Rembrandt's genius, died in the simple house where he himself later died. The artist, his 19-year-old son Titus and Cornelia, his eight-year-old daughter were left alone. This cruel blow of fate caused Rembrandt to retreat even further into his shell. Among the 70-odd self-portraits that remain, those of his last years are among the most vigorous, penetrating and significant. They show the face of a reflective and self-questioning man who is sometimes melancholy but who has gained in strength and wisdom by his victory over grief. The painting is usually fluent and mellow, with warm, rich colours and great strength of form. These characteristics appear in the other, widely varying paintings of this period. Two of the most beautiful works, "The Jewish Bride" and the "Family Group", are outstanding. The background of the first is unfinished and the identity of the two people portrayed has not been established. Here, however, Rembrandt has painted his most moving and sublime picture of conjugal love. The strong red and yellow notes assume a symbolic and psychological value, as is often the case in Rembrandt's later paintings. It is impossible to say whether the title commonly given to the painting is accurate. Certainly its force of expression and colour make it a masterpiece. In the second painting, which resembles the first in style and perception, the artist evokes with deep human emotion the tenderness of family love. There is an almost religious feeling about this portrait which is magnificent as a whole and in its detail.

*Opposite: "The Jewish Bride",
also known as "The Married
Couple", or "Husband and Wife",
c.1668 (Rijksmuseum, Amsterdam).
Some historians have tried to
identify the characters as the
Jewish poet Don Miguel de
Barrios and his wife Abigael de
Pina, or as Titus and his wife,
or Biblical characters such as
Boaz and Ruth. Above: "Family
Group", c.1668 (Herzog Anton
Ulrich Museum, Brunswick).
Below, far left: "Venus and Cupid",
c.1657. The classical subject provides
an opportunity for a portrait of
Hendrickje and the baby Cornelia.
Left: the last self-portrait by
Rembrandt, 1668 (Germanisches
Nationalmuseum, Cologne).*

A SOLITARY DEATH IN DIGNIFIED POVERTY

Below: "Return of the Prodigal Son", 1668 (Hermitage, Leningrad). This theme, used on other occasions, appealed to Rembrandt at the end of his life and it is significant that he should then take it up again. The painting reveals great compassion and is regarded as among his finest works. Opposite: "Self-portrait" (Mauritshuis, The Hague).

In 1668 two events occurred in swift succession. Titus married Magdalena van Loo and left his father's house, and then, one month after his marriage, the young man died. This was yet another grievous blow to Rembrandt who had always dearly loved Titus, his only surviving son by Saskia. It has been suggested that Saskia's and Titu's ill-health were caused by an infection passed on by Rembrandt, but this cannot be proved. After Titus's death Magdalena had a daughter in 1669 whom she called Titia, in remembrance of her husband, but Magdalena herself died on October 21 of the same year. Cornelia van Rijn, Hendrickje's daughter, married the painter Cornelius Suythof on May 30, 1670, after her father's death. In 1673 in Batavia in the Dutch East Indies, she had a son who was christened Rembrandt in honour of his famous grandfather. Cornelia was with her father in the last days of his life, at the house in the Rozengracht opposite the Nieuwe Doolhof. Perhaps she was by his side when he died on October 4 1669. On October 8 he was buried at the Westerkerk (West Church). An inventory drawn up after his death gives a clear picture of the way he had been living. Apart from 19 paintings, some of which were unfinished, he had little furniture or linen. In the "best" bedroom there was a bed with a straw mattress, five pillows, two covers, six silk bed-curtains, a silk coverlet, four green window-curtains, a small table of oak, with a cloth, a mirror, a chair and an iron plate. He obviously lived in a state of dignified poverty. Mainly, however, we see a man of genius who was consciously paying for his own faults and the faults of others toward himself, those who, despite having acclaimed him and made him wealthy, frequently did not appreciate him and finally abandoned him without pity. Quite alone, having lost all those he loved, Rembrandt somehow found the strength in the midst of grief and solitude, to reach even greater heights and to analyse himself and the world about him ever more deeply. He left a great pictorial poem to the world, 650 paintings, 300 etchings and 2,000 drawings: a great gift to mankind.

Rembrandt was basically a portrait painter, both by inclination and in response to the atmosphere and demands of his time. He painted 415 portraits, among them many self-portraits. Of his paintings, 142 were inspired by Old and New Testament themes, 25 by mythological and historical stories, and 29 were "genre" paintings. His was an anti-classical spirit which was at once profoundly realistic and imaginative. His composition and treatment of colour were strikingly new. He enriched the chiaroscuro technique of Caravaggio in an increasingly personal way. His emotional involvement in his subject was always expressed with incomparable variety and intensity of feeling through the medium of form and colour which, with his increasing mastery, he made more original, vigorous and spiritual. He was a brilliant draughtsman and an engraver of genius. In his etchings he obtained magnificent effects from the interplay of black and white. His contemporaries, although admiring him, never understood his courageous and revolutionary genius. They criticized him for ignoring the "rules of beauty" without realising that he was creating a beauty which was not based on aesthetic rules but on the spiritual grandeur of his observation of nature and man.

1606– July 15: Birth of Rembrandt Harmenszoon van Rijn, fifth of seven children of a wealthy miller, at Leyden.

1609– Foundation of the Bank of Amsterdam.

1610– Death of Michelangelo da Caravaggio.

1620– The young Rembrandt abandons his studies to take up art. After three years' apprenticeship he leaves Leyden for Amsterdam where he studies under Pieter Lastman who was directly influenced by the Carracci and indirectly by Caravaggio.

1621– Foundation of the Dutch East Indies Company.

1625– Rembrandt returns to his home town and sets up a studio. The "Leyden period" begins, first of the five periods into which his artistic life is divided; this period lasts until 1630. Hugo Grotius in his *De jure belli ac pacis* establishes the basis for international law.

1626– Rembrandt paints "Tobit and Anna with a Kid" and "Balaam's Ass". Foundation of New Amsterdam (subsequently New York) which becomes the centre of Dutch possessions in North America.

1627– Rembrandt paints "St. Paul in Prison".

1631– Rembrandt settles in Amsterdam which he never leaves again. He paints "Portrait of Nicolaes Ruts" and "The Holy Family".

1632– He paints "The Anatomy Lesson". He becomes famous as a portrait painter through his great psychological insight.

1634– He marries Saskia van Uylenburch. He records her appearance in "Portrait of Saskia" and "Self-portrait with Saskia". She later acted as model for many of his paintings.

1636– Foundation of the University of Utrecht. Two very different paintings, "The Blinding of Samson" and "Danae", were executed in this year. The "first" Amsterdam period ends and the "second" begins. It lasts until 1642, the year of his wife's death. During this period he is commissioned by Prince Frederick Henry of Orange to paint a series of pictures representing scenes of the Passion ("Crucifixion", "Descent from the Cross", etc.).

1640– The Dutch gain the monopoly of European trade with Japan. Death of Rembrandt's mother, of whom many portraits can still be seen.

1640-50– Rembrandt's finest etchings were made in these years. Among the most famous are "The Three Trees" and "Christ Healing the Sick", also called the "Hundred-Guilder Print" because copies of it were sold for that price.

1641– Birth of Titus, the only one of Rembrandt's and Saskia's four sons to survive childhood.

1642– He paints "The Night Watch". June 14, his wife dies. The "third" Amsterdam period, characterized by reflection and balance begins, and lasts until c.1656.

1646– In this year he paints only "The Adoration of the Shepherds" the first of the Passion series. He had painted the Crucifixion in 1636.

1647– "Susanna and the Elders".

1648– "Christ at Emmaus". The Treaty of Westphalia finally ratifies the independence of Holland.

1649– Geertige Direx who had gone to live with Rembrandt after his wife's death brings an action for breach of promise against him. Meanwhile a young girl, Hendrickje Stoffels, who was to be the artist's faithful companion and model, until her death, had entered the household.

1651– "Girl at the Window" perhaps a portrait of the young Hendrickje.

1654– He paints "Bathsheba" with Hendrickje as model.

1656– Birth of Cornelia, daughter of Rembrandt and Hendrickje Stoffels whose position in the Rembrandt household was never legalized.

1657– His house is sold and the valuable collection of *objets d'art* and curios which Rembrandt had gradually acquired, and which were in part the cause of his ruin, were put up for auction. From this year until his death is known as the "fourth" Amsterdam period, during which time he painted such masterpieces as "The Jewish Bride" and "The Family Group".

1661– Given the task of decorating one lunette of the gallery in the new Town Hall of Amsterdam; he begins "The Plot of Claudius Civilis" which he finishes two years later. The canvas is not accepted.

1662– He paints "The Members of the Clothmakers' Guild" or "The Staalmeesters". Hendrickje dies.

1668– Titus, the painter's son dies shortly after his marriage.

1669– The last self-portrait. October 4, death of Rembrandt.

THE
ROYAL
YEAR
1990

PHOTOGRAPHED BY
TIM GRAHAM

MICHAEL O'MARA BOOKS LIMITED

Above left, above and right: On 4 August the Duke and Duchess of York and their little daughter Princess Beatrice embarked on the Royal Yacht Britannia at Portsmouth at the start of the Queen's traditional annual cruise to the Western Isles of Scotland. The Princess who was to celebrate her first birthday on board a few days later delighted the waiting crowds with cheerful smiles and waves.

Left: On the way north to Scotland the Royal Yacht Britannia paid a visit to the Isle of Man on 8 August where the Queen carried out several official engagements with the Duke of Edinburgh.

Far left and left: The Princess of Wales and Prince William and Prince Henry arriving at Aberdeen airport on 14 August from where they drove to nearby Balmoral Castle for the start of the royal family's summer holiday. The Prince of Wales had already joined the rest of the royal party on board the Royal Yacht Britannia.

Below: The Prince and Princess of Wales leaving Wetherby, Prince William's pre-preparatory school in Notting Hill, London after taking him back to school on 7 September, the first day of the new school year.

On 10 September the Princess
of Wales visited the Burghley
Horse Trials in Lincolnshire
where she presented the prizes
to the winning British team.
In a clean sweep all three
individual medals were also won
by British riders.

On 11 September Prince Henry began as a new boy at Prince William's school, Wetherby, four days late as he had been ill at the beginning of term. On his first morning he was very keen to make up for lost time, and eagerly greeted the headmistress, Miss Frederika Blair-Turner.

Below: A keen tennis player herself, the Princess of Wales visited Bisham Abbey in Buckinghamshire on 13 September to open the Lawn Tennis Association's National Training Centre. Right: On 12 September the Duchess of York was the guest of honour at a Foyles Literary Luncheon in London for the publication of her children's books about Budgie the helicopter. Earlier that morning Buckingham Palace had announced that the Duchess was expecting her second child in the spring and she was in radiant mood as she arrived for the lunch. Far right: On 14 September the Princess of Wales as patron of the British Lung Foundation attended the launch of the charity's Snowball Coffee Mornings at Claridge's, London.

In the absence of any grand
royal wedding in 1989, the
marriage of Viscount Althorp,
Earl Spencer's son and brother
to the Princess of Wales, to Miss
Victoria Lockwood, a former
model, was seen by the public
as the next best thing, and the
eighteenth-style ceremony
was meticulously planned.
The marriage took place on
16 September at Great
Brington, near Althorp,
the Spencer family home
in Northamptonshire.
Below: The couple
photographed in the grounds
of Althorp shortly after their
engagement was announced.
Right: The Princess of Wales
with her mother, the Hon.
Mrs Shand-Kydd at the
wedding. Far right: The Prince
and Princess of Wales arriving at
the church with Prince William.

This page: Prince Henry and his cousin Alexander Fellowes were the two page boys at the wedding. They were dressed in eighteenth-century style costume, directly copied from a portrait of a former Viscount Althorp by Sir Joshua Reynolds which hangs at Althorp. Facing page: Even the torrential rain couldn't dampen the happiness of the bride and groom as they posed for photographs outside the church with their bridesmaids and page boys, all of whom were nieces and nephews of Viscount Althorp. From left to right are Eleanor Fellowes, Prince Henry, Alexander Fellowes and Emily McCorquodale.

Left: On 18 September the Princess of Wales attended the memorial service at Southwark Cathedral, London for those lost in the Marchioness *pleasure boat disaster in August when fifty-one people drowned in the river Thames.*

Facing page: On 19 September the Princess of Wales attended a charity performance of the musical, Miss Saigon *at the Theatre Royal, Drury Lane. The performance was in aid of the Prince's Trust.*

Left and facing page above: On 20 September the Princess of Wales visited the headquarters of Weetabix Limited at Burton Latimer in Northamptonshire where she donned white coat and hat to visit the factory. Right: On 26 September, looking stunning in pink check with a matching hat, the Princess of Wales attended a Service of Thanksgiving and unveiled a new North Transept Window in St Albans Cathedral, Hertfordshire.

THE QUEEN IN SINGAPORE AND MALAYSIA

9 – 21 October 1989

The Queen and the Duke of Edinburgh travelled to the Far East in October to attend the opening stages of the bi-annual Commonwealth Heads of Government Meeting which was to take place in Malaysia. Before the Meeting the royal couple made a state visit to the prosperous city-state of Singapore, which the Queen had last visited in 1972, followed by a three-day state visit to Malaysia. The Queen was greeted by enthusiastic crowds throughout the colourful tour which was a great success.

Left and right: At the state banquet in Singapore with the Prime Minister of Singapore, Mr Lee Kuan Yew. With her striking gold embroidered dress the Queen is wearing Queen Mary's diamond tiara.

Below left and below: The Queen and Prince Philip had a varied programme in Singapore, including a colourful visit to a local school in Tanjong Pegar, the city's Chinatown.

Every state visit abroad includes a garden party for the local British community. In Singapore the garden party took place in the High Commissioner's residence and 2000 guests eagerly lined up to greet the Queen. Because of the stifling heat, the men were allowed to dispense with their jackets, a very rare occurrence on royal occasions.

Facing page: The Queen on board the Royal Yacht Britannia *for the Return Dinner for the President of Singapore and Mrs Wee. Right: Inspecting the guard of honour at the arrival ceremony in Parliament Square in Kuala Lumpur, the capital of Malaysia. In Asia yellow is the royal colour and large yellow umbrellas were used to protect the Queen from the fierce sun. Below: For the visit to the Shah Alam Mosque, one of the largest in Asia, the Queen donned an embroidered coat and matching slippers in accordance with Moslem custom.*

The Queen and Prince Philip being guided around the magnificent main courtyard and prayer hall of Shah Alam Mosque by the Amman.

The royal banquet in the Queen's honour took place at the Istana Negara palace. The host was the Yang di-Pertuan Agong (or king), who is Sultan Azlan Shah. The Agong is elected for a period of five years and is chosen by the country's sultans from among their number.

Facing page above right and this page right: On the Sunday afternoon of their visit to Kuala Lumpur the Queen and Prince Philip paid a visit to the Selangor Turf Club where they watched the racing. Facing page above left and below: On the last day of the state visit to Malaysia the Queen and Prince Philip had lunch with the Agong at Istana Iskandariah, the palace of the Sultan of Penang.

Left: The walkabout at Ipoh airport before returning to Kuala Lumpur at the end of the state visit. Below: The official gifts presented by the Queen and Prince Philip to their Malay hosts, a carriage clock and two magnificent signed photographs. Far below: The Queen at the opening of the new British High Commission in Kuala Lumpur.

A VISIT TO INDONESIA AND HONG KONG

3 – 10 November 1989

The exotic sights and sounds of South-East Asia awaited the Prince and Princess of Wales when they made official visits to Indonesia and Hong Kong in November. The visit to Indonesia got off to an auspicious start when the President's witch doctors were ordered to ensure fine weather for the tour and a heavy downpour of tropical rain obligingly stopped just before the royal couple flew in from London.

This page: The Princess of Wales created a lasting impression on the people of Indonesia when she visited the Sitanala Leprosy Hospital on the outskirts of Jakarta. She shook hands with many of the leprosy victims.
Facing page: Joining in the fun at the leprosy hospital.

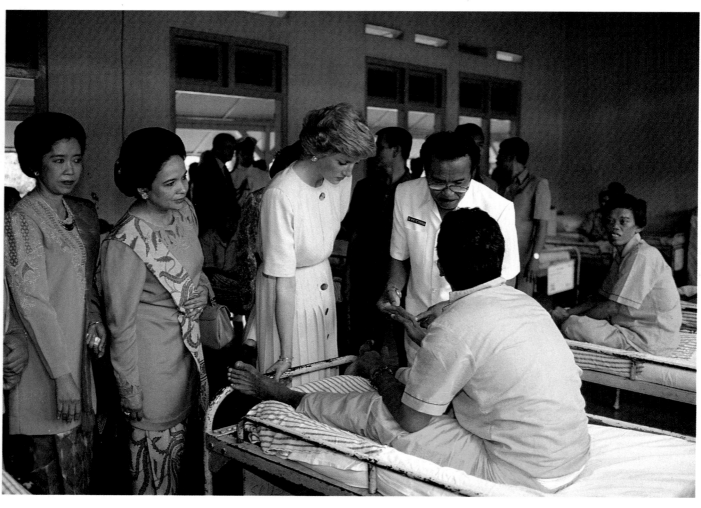

Facing page above: At the end of her visit to the Sitanala Leprosy Hospital the Princess of Wales was persuaded to have a go at a game of bowls in the hospital grounds. Facing page below: Receiving a gift from the hospital inmates. Right: During their short visit to Indonesia the Prince and Princess of Wales were able to catch a glimpse of the traditional Indonesian way of life when they visited Taman Mini, a beautiful park with replica houses built in traditional style which contain displays of different handicrafts from Indonesia's many islands.

Left: The Prince and Princess of Wales touring the Indonesian cultural park, Taman Mini. Below: The Princess of Wales admiring magnificent traditional Indonesian costumes at Taman Mini.

This page: The Prince of Wales at the Commonwealth War Graves Cemetery in Jakarta where he laid a wreath in remembrance of those who had died in the Second World War.

During their visit to Indonesia the Prince and Princess of Wales were received by the Sultan of Yogyakarta and his family at the Karaton Palace in the old provincial capital of Yogyakarta in southern Java. Here in the stifling heat they watched a programme of traditional Javanese dancing.

Left: The Prince of Wales visiting the eighth-century Borobudur Temple in southern Java which is one of the national symbols of Indonesia. It is the largest Buddhist temple outside India and lay hidden for centuries in the jungle until re-discovered only a century ago. Prince Charles climbed to the top to touch a special statue of Buddha inside the dome which is supposed to bring good fortune to those who touch it. Below: The Prince and Princess of Wales viewing traditional handicraft displays at Yogyakarta. Facing page: For the arrival in Hong Kong the Princess of Wales wore a stunning purple and red silk suit designed by Catherine Walker with a matching Chinese-style silk hat.

Despite the political tensions between the British government and the people of Hong Kong, fearful of what Chinese rule will bring in mid-1997, the Prince and Princess of Wales were warmly welcomed during their busy three days in Hong Kong. *Facing page above:* The Princess of Wales playing a fishing game at the Tuen Mun District Festival. *Facing page far left:* The Prince of Wales visiting the Central and Western District in the older part of Hong Kong island. *Facing page left:* The Princess of Wales wearing flower garlands presented by Gurkha wives at the naval headquarters, HMS Tamar. *Right:* The Princess of Wales at the opening ceremony for the new Hong Kong Cultural Centre in Kowloon. With the dazzling beaded evening dress and jacket the Princess wears the pearl and diamond tiara given to her by the Queen as a wedding present in 1981.

Previous pages: The Queen on her way to Westminster for the State Opening of Parliament on 21 November.

Left: The Princess Royal in Hyde Park on 16 November to open a manège and children's playground. Below left: A few days later on 21 November the Princess Royal, as Patron of the Spinal Injuries Association, attended the Coral Gala Ball at the Café Royal. Below right: Princess Michael of Kent at the Sparks Charity Ball at the Hilton Hotel on 5 December.

Right: Prince and Princess Michael of Kent dancing at the Sparks Charity Ball. Below left: As President, the Queen Mother is a regular attender of the Royal Smithfield Show, the big agricultural show held at Earl's Court, London in early December each year. She is herself an owner of pedigree livestock at the Castle of Mey, her home in north Scotland. Below right: Princess Michael of Kent talking to the boxer, Frank Bruno after watching him play the part of Aladdin in the Christmas pantomime at the Dominion Theatre, London.

Both pages: A new series of photographs of the Duke and Duchess of Gloucester taken at Barnwell Manor, their country home in Northamptonshire. Left: The Duke and Duchess of Gloucester with their children (from left to right) the Lady Rose Windsor, the Lady Davina Windsor and the Earl of Ulster.

Facing page left: On 11 January the Princess of Wales visited the Thomas Coram Foundation's Homeless Children's Project in Camden, London. Facing page right: As President, the Princess of Wales visited the Royal Marsden Hospital in Sutton, Surrey on 29 January.

Left: The Princess of Wales, Patron of RELATE National Marriage Guidance, visited the organization's Marriage Guidance Office in Ipswich, Suffolk on 1 February. Below: She visited another of their offices on 6 February, this time in Oxford where she carried out several other engagements as well.

Facing page and left: On 9 February the Duchess of York as Patron presented the awards for the Combined Services Skiing Championships in Megève in the French Alps. Expecting her second child not long afterwards, the Duchess was determined to carry out her duties as Patron and visited the championships even though this year she was unable to do any skiing herself. Below left and right: In mid-January the Duchess of York took Princess Beatrice to Klosters in Switzerland for her first taste of winter sports.

Facing page left: On 7 February the Princess of Wales accompanied the Prince of Wales to the charity première of the film, Steel Magnolias in aid of the Prince's Trust. Facing page right above and below: On 13 February the Princess of Wales had a busy day in Wales, visiting the Welsh Porcelain Company Limited in Maesteg as well as other engagements in Mid-Glamorgan.

Right: The Princess of Wales, President of the Royal Marsden Hospital, visited the hospital in South Kensington, London on 21 February to attend the launch of the hospital's appeal.

Facing page above left and below: The end of February saw terrible storms in Britain which caused great damage up and down the country, including the flooding of hundreds of homes at Towyn in north Wales. On 1 March, St David's Day, the Prince and Princess of Wales visited the flood victims camping out at their temporary home, Bodelwyddan Castle.

Facing page above right, right and below: On 7 March the Duke and Duchess of Kent carried out a series of engagements in Leicester, including visiting the Ash Field School for the Disabled.

OFFICIAL VISITS TO NIGERIA AND CAMEROON

15 – 23 March 1990

The Prince and Princess of Wales's visit to Nigeria was the first by the royal family since the country gained independence from Britain in 1960 and followed the President's state visit to Britain in May 1989. The welcome they received was almost as warm as the blazing West African climate and in between the official engagements they relaxed on the Royal Yacht Britannia.

This page: The Princess of Wales on the first day of the official visit to Nigeria. Facing page: Only three hours after arriving in Lagos, the Princess of Wales was on her way to the state banquet given in their honour by the President and Mrs Babangida.

The President's wife, Mrs Babangida, works hard to improve the life of the millions of poor young rural-dwelling Nigerian women and on the second day of the visit she took the Princess of Wales to an outdoor fair organized by the 'Better Life for Rural Women' movement. There the Princess received gifts from local women dressed in tribal costume.

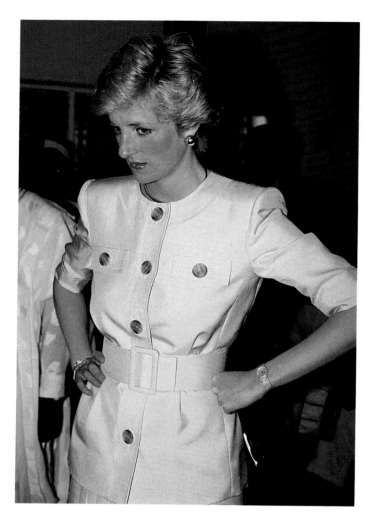

This page: The Prince and the Princess of Wales visiting the leprosy ward at the Molai Centre, a bush hospital at Maiduguri in north-east Nigeria, a region badly affected by leprosy. As they toured the crowded ward the Princess of Wales charmed everyone by her relaxed manner and her insistence on greeting the patients with handshakes.

Facing page: The Prince and Princess of Wales arriving in Enugu in eastern Nigeria where they watched a series of tribal dances, almost a daily feature of life in West Africa.

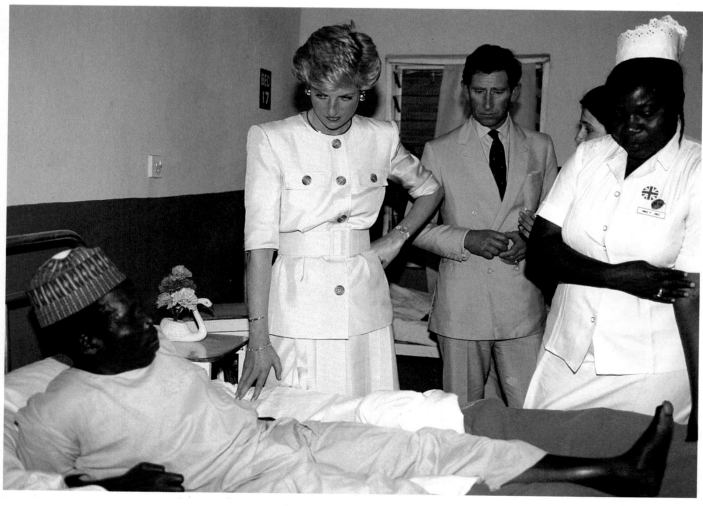

Previous pages and above: In contrast to the hospital visits which showed the Princess the harsh side of life in Africa the displays of traditional dancing illustrated the exotic side and came as light relief. The Princess of Wales was fascinated by the wonderful tribal costumes worn by the women and children.

Left: The Princess of Wales signing the visitors' book at the Lagos University Teaching Hospital, where Prince Charles presented the hospital with an incubator as a token of Britain's current large aid package to Nigeria. Facing page: The Princess of Wales in striking pink and yellow silk at the start of the official visit to Cameroon, a former French colony and Nigeria's eastern neighbour.

Left and below left: For the Princess the first day of engagements in Yaoundé, the capital of Cameroon, included an audience with the president's wife, Mrs Biya and a visit to a centre for deaf and mute children.

Below and facing page: The Princess of Wales arriving at the state banquet at the Palais de l'Unité in Yaoundé.

In between the formal engagements the Prince and Princess of Wales managed to catch a brief glimpse of real West Africa. Right: At Umnagbai in Nigeria the way of life for the local farming community has hardly changed for centuries. Below: The Prince of Wales, whose concern for the world's endangered environment is well known, paid a visit to Korup in the north-west highlands of Cameroon, one of the largest protected areas of virgin rainforest in the world.

Facing page: The Prince and Princess of Wales at Bamenda in Cameroon.

On the evening of 23 March the Duchess of York gave birth to her second child at the Portland Hospital in London. The Duke of York, an officer in the Royal Navy, was on duty at the Portland naval base over 200 miles from London and only arrived shortly before the birth. *Above left and left:* Princess Beatrice paid several visits to the Portland to see her mother and new sister and (left) on Mothering Sunday took the Duchess of York a special posy of flowers. *Above:* The Princess of Wales was one of the first visitors to the Portland Hospital, rushing there on Sunday morning soon after arriving home from her tour of West Africa.

Right and below: The Duchess of York leaving hospital on 30 March with the one-week-old Princess of York whose names were announced later as Eugenie Victoria Helena. The Duke and Duchess of York obviously have a preference for Victorian names as, like Beatrice, the name they gave their first child, Eugenie, Victoria and Helena were all names given to members of Queen Victoria's family.

The Princess of Wales enjoyed an Easter holiday with her children on the Caribbean island of Necker. Invited by the Princess to join in the large family party were her two sisters, Lady Sarah McCorquodale who brought two of her children, George and Emily, and Lady Jane Fellowes, with her children Alexander, Laura and Eleanor, her mother, the Hon. Mrs Shand-Kydd and her brother Viscount Althorp and his new wife. On the third day of the holiday the Princess invited photographers to come and take pictures, but only from a safe distance offshore. The royal party's privacy on the island itself was respected. High spirits on the beach included burying the Princess of Wales in the sand.

The traditional Easter Day Service at St George's Chapel, Windsor was attended by the Queen and other members of the royal family. The Princess of Wales and the two young princes did not attend as their return flight from the Caribbean had been delayed by eight hours and they had only arrived at the castle earlier that morning. *Right*: The Prince of Wales with his cousin Viscount Linley. *Below*: The Duchess of York and Viscount Linley. This was the Duchess's first public appearance since leaving hospital two weeks earlier with her new born baby, Princess Eugenie.

Below: The Princess Royal and her children Zara and Peter returning to the castle after the Easter Day service. *Facing page*: The Dean of Windsor escorts the Queen and the Queen Mother to their cars after the service.

Right: On 19 April Princess Alexandra carried out several engagements in Sussex, including opening a new Convalescent Rest Building of the Fire Services National Benevolent Fund at Littlehampton. Below: The Princess of Wales had a busy day in Leicestershire on 24 April. In Loughborough she carried out engagements as President of Barnardo's and Patron of the English Women's Indoor Bowling Association and had lunch at Ladybird Books.

Facing page: It was back to school the next day for Prince William and Prince Henry for the start of the summer term and Prince William's last at Wetherby School in Notting Hill before moving on to prep school in September.

Facing page far left: Princess Margaret wore striking red damask for her visit to Crowborough in East Sussex on 25 April to open the Horder Centre for Arthritics's new Orthopaedic Centre. Left: The next day the Duchess of Kent carried out engagements in a rainswept High Wycombe, Buckinghamshire including performing the opening ceremony of the new training centre of the 5th (Volunteer) Battalion The Royal Green Jackets. Facing page below: The Duchess of Kent, the long-standing Patron of Age Concern England, then went on to open a new Age Concern Day Centre near High Wycombe as part of the charity's Golden Jubilee celebrations. At the Centre the Duchess was invited to join the staff and guests for tea and showing her usual concern for other people with the minimum of fuss, she ended up passing round the cakes herself.

Left: Princess Alice, Duchess of Gloucester celebrates her ninetieth birthday in 1991, one year after the Queen Mother, her sister-in-law. Like the Queen Mother, she still carries out engagements up and down the country and on 2 May, as Patron of the Girls' Public Day School Trust, she opened the Junior School Building at St Helen's School, Northwood in Middlesex. Below left: Wearing a striking blue evening suit the Princess of Wales went to the Royal Albert Hall in London on 25 April for a gala charity performance of Phil Collins in Concert in aid of the Prince's Trust. Below right: On 27 April the Princess of Wales went to north London to open the Depaul Trust Oblique Housing for Homeless Youth Centre where she met Cardinal Basil Hume.

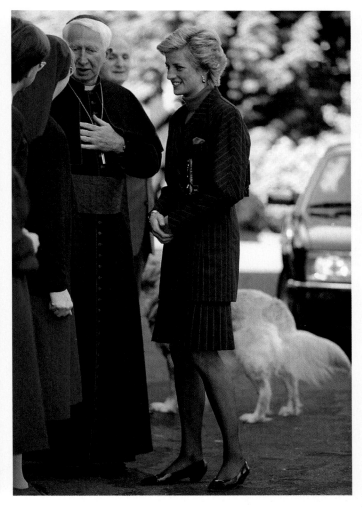

This page: Polo has always been one of Prince Charles's favourite ways of keeping fit. On 24 May at Cirencester Park in Gloucestershire he had Prince William and Prince Henry to help him prepare for the match. The princes also amused themselves by playing with short polo sticks and it won't be all that long before Prince Charles starts to teach them the skills of the game. He himself was taught to play polo by Prince Philip who was an extremely accomplished player until arthritis forced him to give it up in the early 1970s. Facing page: The Princess of Wales as Patron of Turning Point, visited the charity's Lorne House drugs project for young people in the East End of London on 3 May.

Left and right: The Prince
and Princess of Wales arriving
at Budapest airport on 7 May
where they were met by
President Gonoz. During the
short welcoming ceremony
Prince Charles inspected a guard
of honour. Facing page above:
The Princess of Wales arriving
for the official dinner given
in their honour that evening
at Parliament. Overleaf: The
following morning the Princess
of Wales accompanied Prince
Charles to Budapest's
University of Economic Sciences
where he delivered an
impassioned speech on the evils
of communism. Surrounded by
excited crowds, they then
walked to the city's Central
Market with its crowded stalls
piled high with colourful foods
for a spot of sightseeing.

HISTORIC VISIT
TO HUNGARY

7 – 10 May 1990

The Prince and Princess of Wales made the first official royal visit to Eastern Europe when they arrived in Budapest for a four-day visit to Hungary. The country's first democratic elections for over forty years had taken place in April and the Hungarians gave the royal couple an emotional welcome as their visit set a seal of approval on the country's break from communist rule.

Right and below: While in Budapest the Princess of Wales spent a morning at the world-renowned Peto Institute which has pioneered the highly successful treatment of cerebral palsy through conductive education. Over 500 children live at the Institute at any one moment, including up to 100 British children whose parents have often made great sacrifices to accompany their children to Budapest for treatment. The Princess was deeply moved by what she saw and chatted and laughed with the patients, who included nine-year-old Dawn Charlton (right) from Nottinghamshire who has spent three years at the Institute learning to read, write and walk.

Facing page: Leaving Budapest for a day, the Prince and Princess of Wales travelled to Bugacz in the Great Hungarian Plain, a region famed for farming and breeding horses. In order to see the countryside and visit a simple peasant farmhouse they exchanged their official car for a horse-drawn carriage. Driving them was the Hungarian world carriage-driving champion Lazsle Juahaz.

Facing page and right: While at the Peto Institute the Princess of Wales held her first investiture on behalf of the Queen and presented the Director, Dr Maria Hari with an honorary Order of the British Empire Medal or OBE for her work at the Institute since its founding. Above left: The last few hours of the royal visit to Budapest included a short river cruise on the Danube and a walkabout in the old city centre. Above right: Prince Charles enjoying a glass of the local schnapps in Hungary.

The Royal Windsor Horse Show
takes place in the middle of May
in the spectacular setting
of the Home Park at the foot
of Windsor Castle. The Queen
always attends, often
accompanied by members of her
family. Prince Philip is an
expert driver and, as in
previous years, competed in
the International Driving Grand
Prix, a three-day event for
carriage-driving. To watch
Prince Philip compete in the
marathon event the Queen
brought along the Duke and
Duchess of York and Princess
Beatrice.

The Duchess of York with
Princess Beatrice at the
Royal Windsor Horse Show.
They were watching Prince
Philip compete in the marathon
event of the Driving Grand Prix.

Facing page above: The Duchess of Kent meeting diplomats' children in national costume on 16 May at the 31st International Spring Fair at Kensington Town Hall. The Fair is organized each year by wives in the diplomatic community in London to raise money for charity. Facing page below: The following day the Queen went to Salisbury Plain in Wiltshire to visit the 5th Airborne Brigade to mark the 50th Anniversary of the Airborne Forces.

Right: The Princess of Wales went with Prince Charles, Patron of the Abbeyfield Society, to the Central Hall, Westminster on 15 May to attend the Society's Annual General Meeting.

In June the Princess Royal paid the first official visit by a member of the royal family to the Soviet Union since the Russian Revolution.
Left: Only two hours after her arrival, the Princess Royal was greeted by President Gorbachev at the Kremlin. Right: The highly successful thirteen day-visit included a wreath-laying ceremony in the city of Volgograd which lost two million dead in World War Two and fabulous sightseeing in Moscow's Red Square.

Below: The Princess Royal addressing students at Moscow State University. After the frank 'questions and answers' session the Princess was given a standing ovation. Below right: Watching a performance of Giselle at the Bolshoi Theatre.

Left: The Princess of Wales as Patron attended a charity gala at Sadler's Wells Theatre in London on 5 June in aid of Turning Point. Right: The Queen and Queen Mother were well wrapped up at Derby Day, the coldest and wettest for over 100 years.

Below: The Duchess of York, President of the Hackney Horse Society, inspecting sheep at the society's 100th annual show at Ardingly in West Sussex on 7 June. Below right: On the following day as Patron of the Motor Neurone Disease Association she attended a lunch and opened new staff accommodation at the Bell Inn, Aston Clinton in Buckinghamshire.

Above and right: The Duke and Duchess of York as Patrons of the York Minster Trust visited the city of York on 15 June for the Service of Dedication of the Restored Stonework of the Great West Window.

Left: On 14 June the Princess of Wales had a full day of engagements in the High Peak district of Derbyshire, including touring the Swizzels Matlow sweet factory at New Mills.

Trooping the Colour, the colourful ceremony held every June to mark the sovereign's official birthday, is one of the highlights of the summer in London. Far left: Elaborate rehearsals are held beforehand and at the official dress rehearsal the Prince of Wales, wearing the uniform of colonel of the Welsh Guards, took the salute in place of the Queen. Left: The following Saturday, 16 June was the Queen's Official Birthday and here the Queen Mother is accompanied by the Princess of Wales, Prince William and Prince Henry on her way to Horse Guards Parade to watch Trooping the Colour. Below: Prince Henry snatching a quick ride on his father's horse in the inner courtyard of Buckingham Palace. Below left: The Queen returning to Buckingham Palace after the parade is over. Below right: The royal family watching the spectacular flypast by the Royal Air Force from the palace balcony. Overleaf: The Queen taking the final salute in the forecourt of Buckingham Palace.

Left: After Trooping the Colour was over the Prince of Wales relaxed by playing a hard game of polo at the Guards Polo Club, Windsor. Below: Unfortunately, less than two weeks later he broke his right arm badly when he fell off his horse while playing polo at Cirencester. He is seen here leaving hospital on 1 July, the Princess of Wales's birthday, in time for a quiet dinner at Highgrove.

Facing page: This year's Royal Ascot was well attended by the royal family. Above left: The Queen Mother and Princess Margaret making their way through the crowds followed by the Duke of Gloucester and the Duke and Duchess of Kent. Above right: On the first day the Princess of Wales wore a striking red and purple suit. Below: Walking through the royal enclosure on the first day are the Prince and Princess of Wales, the Duke and Duchess of York and Viscount Linley.

The royal carriage procession before the start of each day's racing is one of the highlights of Royal Ascot. Above: On the opening day of the royal meeting the Queen and Prince Philip are accompanied by the Prince of Wales and the Earl of Westmorland, Master of the Horse. Facing page above: The Queen Mother and the Princess of Wales arriving by carriage on the second day of Royal Ascot. Walking through the crowds at Royal Ascot are (right) the Queen, (centre right) the Prince and Princess of Wales and (far right) the Princess Royal.

Above left and right: The Queen and Prince Philip arriving in Iceland on 25 June for a three-day state visit. Their host was the charming and highly popular President Vigdis Finnbogadottir. Left: The Queen wore her famous Russian fringe tiara for the state banquet in Reykjavik. Facing page above: The overall mood of the state visit was relaxed and the Queen was able to do some informal sightseeing, including meeting a genuine Iceland dog.

Facing page below: The Duchess of York as Patron takes a great interest in the work of the Motor Neurone Disease Association and in the summer she attended several events connected with the charity, including a polo match at the Royal County of Berkshire Polo Club on 18 July.

Opposite page: On 27 June the Queen Mother was given a 90th birthday tribute on Horse Guards Parade, London by the armed services and civilian organizations most closely associated with Her Majesty. 6,000 people took part in the parade including the massed bands of all three services. Opposite below: Celebrities appearing in the procession included the actresses Jerry Hall and Susan Hampshire. Above: As Colonel-in-Chief of the Royal Anglian Regiment the Queen Mother visited the First and Third Battalions at Roman Barracks, Colchester where she presented Long Service and Good Conduct medals.

Right: On 19 July the Queen Mother, acompanied by the Queen, Prince Philip and Princess Margaret attended a gala performance at the London Palladium in celebration of her 90th birthday.

On 1 August the Royal Yacht Britannia, *with the Queen* Mother *on board, arrived in the Port of London. Opposite: That afternoon the Queen Mother toured the East End of London where she met 95-year-old Mary Lee. 'Oh, you beat even me', the Queen Mother said. Above: The Queen Mother revisited All Saints Anglican Church where she had comforted the locals during the devastation of the Blitz, 50 years ago. In the evening a banquet was held on* Britannia *in her honour while Tower Bridge was showered in a dramatic firework display. Right: The Princess of Wales arrives at Clarence House on 4 August, the Queen Mother's 90th birthday. Below: The Queen Mother and other members of the royal family greet the crowds outside Clarence House.*

Copyright © 1990 by Tim Graham

First published in Great Britain in 1990 by Michael O'Mara Books Limited,
9 Lion Yard, 11–13 Tremadoc Road, London SW4 7NF
in association with Independent Television News Limited

A CIP catalogue record for this book is available from the British Library

ISBN 1–85479–002–1

Designed by Martin Bristow
Edited by Fiona Holman

Typeset by Florencetype Ltd, Kewstoke, Avon
Printed and bound by Printer Industria Grafica SA, Barcelona, Spain